How to be a Civil Servant

How to be a
Civil Servant

Martin Stanley

POLITICO'S

First published in Great Britain 2000 by
Politico's Publishing, an imprint of
Methuen Publishing Limited
215 Vauxhall Bridge Road
London SW1V 1EJ

A CIP catalogue record for this book is available from the British Library.

ISBN 1 84275 097 6

Printed and bound in Great Britain by Mackays of Chatham.

Contents

What the civil service wants, and I always compare it to a rather stupid dog, it wants to do what its master wants and it wants to be loyal to its master and above all it wants to be loved for doing that.

Sir Richard Mottram

Introduction

Working in Whitehall can be great fun, and very rewarding. It is good to work to improve the lives of fellow citizens, you get to influence important decisions, and you get to meet some fascinating people, a good number of them within the civil service. But new arrivals discover that they are subject to a bewildering mixture of rules, procedures and guidance, whilst at the same time they find it very difficult to obtain basic advice about how to do their job. This book and its accompanying website (http://www.civilservant.org.uk) address this problem by providing a thorough introduction to the duties, responsibilities and working practices of Whitehall officials. I hope that both will be found helpful by those interested in understanding the British civil service, as well as those embarking on a Whitehall career.

The book begins by examining civil servants' professional skills, including the best way to work with Ministers and in Europe. It then describes the professional and ethical constraints within which civil servants must work, including giving advice on Parliamentary business, judicial review and so on.   Finally, it gives advice on how to get things done in Whitehall, and in particular how to overcome obstacles to innovation, as well as describing key leadership and management skills.

This second edition incorporates substantial revisions which will help readers meet the challenge of shifting Whitehall's focus from policy advice to delivery. It also takes account of recent developments in Parliamentary procedures and in Europe.

I must make it clear that the views in this book are entirely my own and have not been officially endorsed. All errors and omissions are my responsibility. Indeed, although I believe that most civil servants would agree with most of what I have written, I am equally sure that none would agree with every word. My comments on Ministerial preferences, and on the way in which Ministers and officials work with each other, reflect my general perceptions. I have taken great care to ensure that no part of the text is based on the practice of any particular Minister or official with whom I have worked.

Finally, I recognise that the advice in this book does not directly deal with the challenges facing the vast majority of civil servants who do not work in central departments, but carry out vital work in Executive Agencies and local offices. It also does not deal with the special circumstances of those working in Scotland, Wales or Northern Ireland. I apologise to such colleagues, but I hope that they, too, will find the book interesting, if only because it will tell them something about the working methods of those whose decisions have such a large influence on their working lives.

Martin Stanley
July 2004

1 Working With Ministers

Today's civil service faces a number of new challenges. One was summarised by the Cabinet Office as follows:

> *The public has higher expectations than ever before about the service it is entitled to:*
> * *A fair, universal provision is no longer enough: people expect their personal needs to be addressed.*
> * *'Authority' is increasingly challenged.*
> * *Inadequate provision is not accepted.*
> * *Litigation over failures is increasing.*

Another was summarised by Tony Blair:

> *The principal challenge is to shift focus from policy advice to delivery. Delivery means outcomes. It means project management. It means adapting to new situations and altering rules and practice accordingly. It means working not in traditional departmental silos. It means working naturally with partners outside of Government. It's not that many individual civil servants aren't capable of this. It is that doing it requires a change of operation and of culture that goes to the core of the civil service.*

Whitehall civil servants therefore need to carry out their traditional professional duties within a modern demanding society in a way which will best achieve worthwhile outcomes. We are not employed to 'make policy', or 'to manage'. We are employed to get things done on Ministers' behalf. We need to make sure that every piece of advice, every brief, every management decision, every letter and every meeting takes us a little closer to our Minister's objectives. How better to start this book, therefore, than by looking at our relationship with Ministers, and how to help them achieve their long term goals?

The Three Key Professional Duties
It is vital, when working with Ministers, to recognise that we have three distinct professional duties. We need to be clear which duty we are carrying out at any one time, for each requires different skills and behaviour. Our three duties are as follows:

First, civil servants give advice to Ministers before they make policy decisions. We must give them private, honest, informed advice and we are expected to face them with the truth even when it turns up in an inconvenient form. The Civil Service Code says that says that the role of the civil service is to assist the government of the day with integrity, honesty, impartiality and objectivity. Put another way, we are employed to 'speak truth unto power'.

Second, we must help Ministers promote and defend their decisions, even if we advised against them. We must, when operating in this mode, now pay much more attention to the tone and impact of what Ministers say and do, rather than focusing on the detail that underlies the policy decision. It matters little whether we think Ministers are right or wrong. It is vital that their programmes are professionally promoted and defended if they are to achieve their objectives.

Third, we are responsible for delivery: implementing Ministers' decisions on the ground and possibly drafting the necessary legislation. Again, we become less analytical, and much more proactive. We now focus almost exclusively on ensuring the delivery of worthwhile outcomes, working closely with delivery partners both inside and outside our department. Indeed, although we undoubtedly continue to work for Ministers, we often have to use Ministers (I know no better word) in order to achieve Ministers' own objectives. After all, little is as effective in driving forward a difficult agenda, as a strong Ministerial speech or a well-prepared meeting between a Minister and a Ministerial colleague, or a powerful interest group, or a delivery partner.

By the way, the need to focus on long-term goals does not exempt us from the duty to respect the numerous constraints within which we are forced to work. These constraints are therefore described in some detail later in this book. But our key professional skill is to be innovative in achieving Ministers' objectives without breaking any rules, and without going on about how difficult it all is.

Before going into further detail, let's take a quick look at our clients.

Ministers

The most junior Ministers are Parliamentary Under Secretaries of State, of whom there will be one in a small department and three or four in a large department. They do a great deal of important work, including piloting Bills through Parliament. They also carry out a wide range of representational and other duties, which means that they are always getting up early in the morning to attend events outside London, and then staying in the House until late in the evening to speak in adjournment debates. They take important decisions on individual cases and narrow issues. But they seldom get to take politically important decisions. These are reserved for their seniors.

The second tier of Ministers are Ministers of State, of which there are, again, usually one to three in a department. These Ministers are more experienced and powerful and will handle – or assist Cabinet Ministers with – the more complex and/or politically tricky issues.

Then there are Cabinet Ministers. Most of them are Ministers in charge of departments, but there are others, including the Leader of the House of Lords and the Chief Whip. Very large or important departments also sometimes get a second Minister in the Cabinet. The Chief Secretary, for instance (who negotiates Government expenditure with his or her colleagues) is number two in the Treasury. Cabinet Ministers who are in charge of departments are usually styled 'Secretary of State' except, for instance, for the Chancellor of the Exchequer. The title of the Secretary of State for the Home Department is almost always shortened to 'Home Secretary', and 'Foreign Secretary' is also a shortened form. These men and women are of course very powerful, but there is a pecking order within the Cabinet which varies with the political importance of the Minister's department, and his or her personal clout and experience. But the Chancellor, the Home Secretary and the Foreign Secretary are always very influential, and invariably the top three posts in the pecking order.

The whole structure is headed by the Prime Minister, an analysis of whose role and responsibilities is beyond the scope of this book. Suffice it to say that Prime Ministers have only a limited amount of political capital at their disposal, so they prefer to work through consensus, especially when dealing with senior and powerful colleagues. And as civil servants develop a natural loyalty to their departmental Ministers, the result is that there is no clear pyramid of management responsibility, which can make it difficult to handle cross-departmental issues. However, the strengthening of the Cabinet Office, which took place in the late 1990s, has gone some way towards addressing this problem.

Private Offices

Every Minister is provided with a dedicated life support system known as a Private Office. These offices are a key link in handling Ministerial correspondence, organising the Ministerial diary, conveying Ministers' views to officials, and providing Ministers with information and views from their departments. They therefore play a crucial role in managing two precious commodities for Ministers: information and time. They also play a crucial role in helping the Minister understand – and ask difficult questions about – advice from the department.

It is worth investing a lot of time and effort into working well with Private Offices. Putting on one side the fact that you should want to help them do their jobs, you also want them to think that you are helpful, knowledgeable, sensible and flexible. This is because they will communicate their views to the Minister, in all sorts of subtle ways – and sometimes not so subtle if they really do detest you.

The Minister in charge of the department will have quite a large office – maybe 12 or more staff in a large department – headed by a Principal Private Secretary (PPS). He or she will be a more experienced official, able to act as interlocutor and trouble-shooter with senior departmental officials. The PPS is a handy first point of call if you need urgent help or advice and do not know who else to approach. PPSs are on call 24 hours a day, 365 days a year, and know where all the bodies are buried. For this reason, they are usually promoted when they leave Private Office, myself included.

The officials in charge of other Ministers' offices are known as Private Secretaries, and they are usually quite young, partly because much of the work is essentially straightforward – preparing notes of meetings and so on – and partly because the job offers excellent experience for future senior officials. And although the work is straightforward, that does not mean that it is easy. The Private Secretary has to take a mass of information and paperwork from the department and prepare it so that it is easy for the Minister to assimilate it even in the small hours of the morning. The Private Secretary might therefore highlight certain text, or prepare a summary of a long document, but must not distort the message when doing so.

The same applies when the Private Secretary is communicating the Minister's views to the department, including when preparing a note of a meeting. It is permissible to emphasise particular points and stress any action needed, but it is not permissible to misrepresent, distort or exaggerate the views of the Minister or anyone else. The main exception is that Private Secretaries will generally ignore what lawyers call obiter dicta i.e. things that are said when Ministers, like the rest of us, choose to air their views on a wide range of subjects in the middle of a conversation about a scarcely related subject. These comments can usually safely be ignored – but only if the Private Secretary is sure that the Minister will not, two weeks later, ask what has happened about his decision to relocate a large part of the department to his constituency.

Don't hesitate, by the way, to challenge the accuracy of a note of a meeting, whether prepared by a Private Secretary or someone in the Cabinet Secretariat. Even the first Cabinet Secretary admitted to 'racking his brains to record and report, what he thinks that they think that they ought to have thought.' The result of such a process can easily be wrong, and such meeting notes are usually too important to go uncorrected.

Things can get difficult when the Minister gets angry, because the Private Secretary is then the one that has to transmit that anger to his or her colleagues in the department. They will usually seek to tone down the Minister's comments but they, like the Minister, will run out of patience if officials seem to be ignoring comments and requests. The result is that they will then quote the Minister's actual words. (I once saw a minute which said '. . . as I asked for this well over a year ago . . . if I do not get a paper . . . within a month I shall commission it outside the department.'). If you get something like this then you really are in trouble.

Be aware, however, that some Private Secretaries get ideas well above their station. It can be very helpful if they ask 'idiot boy' questions that might well occur to someone not closely involved in your area, and they can sometimes be helpful in spotting silly mistakes, or by drawing attention to some development or Ministerial view of which you were not aware. Sometimes, however, and sometimes encouraged by their Ministers, they start acting as alternate policy advisers, commenting freely on the merits of your work. Watch out for this, for something has gone badly wrong if a Minister prefers to hear the advice of his Private Secretary to that of the responsible official.

Private Secretaries also control official attendance at Ministers' meetings. Ideally, the Minister will allow four types of official to attend. The first will be the lead official(s) responsible for preparing the advice and implementing any decisions. The second type will be those, such as more senior officials and lawyers, who will provide further useful contributions to the discussion. The third, occasional attenders, will be inexperienced officials who are gaining experience of working with Ministers. They are expected to keep their mouths shut, and can be usefully employed in writing the note of the meeting, thus removing a chore from the Private Secretary. The fourth are press officers, who should be involved in discussing any issue which has a presentational aspect.

In practice, all Ministers get understandably jumpy if too many officials turn up – and it also looks inefficient, especially in meetings with outsiders. The basic rule, therefore, is one official (not counting the Private Secretary or Special Adviser) to each visitor, although you can usually get away with two officials if there is only one visitor. If there are no visitors then each Minister will have their own threshold, which will be communicated to you by the Private Secretary. It can be particularly difficult if the Minister has favourite civil servants, and won't see anyone else, even if they know much more about the subject under discussion. But you have to accept the Minister's decision and there is no point in shouting at the poor Private Secretary who probably hates it as much as you do.

The daily life of a Private Office revolves around 'the box' – the red rectangular box in which the Minister carries his or her homework. Some Ministers, to everyone's amazement, manage to sign all their letters, and respond to all their submissions, when in the office. Others take several boxes home each night and then never touch them. But most plough through one or two boxes, if only because they contain some quite fascinating stuff.

A typical box will contain a red 'immediate' folder of items requiring immediate decision or action, about which the Private Secretary will ask first thing in the morning. Then there will be a diary folder, prepared by the Diary Secretary – a position which can be one of the worst jobs in Whitehall; there are no thanks if everything goes well, but immediate retribution if something goes wrong: 'How could you send me to Wigan North Western when I should have gone to Wigan Wallgate? Didn't you (a 19 year old who has never been north of Wembley Arena) know the difference?' Ministers also accuse novice Diary Secretaries of arranging meetings to which the Minister had not agreed, and so on. They quickly learn never to confirm any engagement without the Minister's signature, preferably in blood.

Diary Secretaries will therefore threaten to maim any official who has the temerity to tell a member of the public that the Minister's diary is free at a certain time. This is because the member of the public will then expect to be able to arrange a meeting at that time and, if the meeting is not then arranged, they will know that the Minister chose not to see them, rather than that the Minister was literally unable to see them. Frequently, therefore, you will be trapped between a member of the public (who cannot understand why it takes more than 30 seconds to check that the Minister is free – have we never heard of telephones and computers?) and the Diary Secretary (who will ensure that nothing in your official life will ever run sweetly again if you dare to commit the Minister without his or her written agreement – which will not be forthcoming for several weeks). What is the best way of handling this problem? I wish I knew.

The rest of the box will contain folders full of submissions, letters for signature, and background information. The last seldom get read (would you read it at one o'clock in the morning?). The letters get signed, if they look sensible, often without the Minister looking at the covering note from officials. So, if the Minister should definitely give some thought to whether he really wants to sign the letter, you must get the Private Secretary to put a big red note on top. Submissions will also get looked at in varying depth, depending upon how sensible the recommendation – at the top of the document – seems to appear. Again, therefore, do not hide a little bombshell in the middle of a submission. You may think that you are protecting your back, but this ploy will cut no ice with the Minister when the unexpected bomb detonates a day or two later.

Ministerial Aides

One or two other interesting species can be found in and around Private Offices. Parliamentary Private Secretaries (confusingly also known as PPSs) are not civil servants but are MPs who help senior Ministers with their Parliamentary duties. They often attend meetings within the department and should be given as much help and information as possible. However, their duties are primarily party political, and they hold no formal office on behalf of the voter or taxpayer. There are therefore obvious limits to the amount of assistance that they can be given by officials and they should only be given otherwise confidential information if it is clearly necessary for the discharge of their Parliamentary and political duties.

All departments have one or more Special Advisers who are personal appointees of the Secretary of State, but employed as temporary civil servants. They give political, presentational and policy advice to Ministers and help write political speeches and articles, or add a political dimension to speeches etc. drafted by officials. They work closely with Private Offices and Press Offices and give advice in parallel with line divisions. Within that broad job description, their role, experience and abilities vary a great deal. One or two can be difficult to work with, but the vast majority are generally helpful and keen to work with officials. You should therefore keep in close touch with Special Advisers on issues which are likely to attract their attention, and you should be ready with advice and information.

Although Special Advisers may attend meetings with outside organisations, and sometimes make speeches on behalf of their Ministers, they do not represent the Government in any formal sense. They may also let you know their Minister's views and work priorities, and may, on behalf of their Minister, ask you to do work of a fact-finding or advisory nature. But they cannot go so far as to give you instructions. Your principal responsibility continues to be to your line management and your Ministers via their Private Offices. Indeed, your advice to Ministers should always be communicated in person or via Private Offices, even if previously seen and/or agreed by a Special Adviser.

Like Private Secretaries, Special Advisers can be an excellent source of advice about Ministers' policy instincts and priorities. It is certainly worth talking to them before putting up any major submission, and it is usually a good idea to give them a chance to comment on your draft. However, do not make the mistake of letting a Special Adviser steer you in a direction which seems unwise. Maybe the Special Adviser's advice will be different to yours, and maybe the Secretary of State will not take your advice, and maybe the Special Adviser will accurately foretell the Secretary of State's decision, but that should not stop you putting up advice in which you believe.

The main difference between permanent civil servants and Special Advisers is that the latter are usually fiercely loyal to their Minister, on whose career they themselves depend, and sensitive to what they perceive as disloyal criticism. For instance, it is quite in order to ask a Private Secretary what on earth caused the Minister to say such and such a thing to a visitor. The Private Secretary will explain what happened, or acknowledge that the Minister made a mistake, and then you can get on and loyally sort out the resultant problem. But if you put the same question to a Special Adviser, they will often go into defensive mode and/or, even worse, tell the Minister what you said, which hardly helps build up a long term relationship. So it is best to give Special Advisers the clear impression that you believe that their Minister walks on water. They will suspect that you are lying, but respect you for it.

You should also watch out for demarcation disputes with Special Advisers. Many Ministers thrive on a steady diet of witty or barn-storming speeches, which civil servants are not equipped to provide. And although we should stand ready to rebut factually incorrect stories, we are not equipped to provide a political rebuttal service which swings into action whenever the Minister is criticised in the media. Both of these tasks should properly fall to Special Advisers, but they are often under enormous pressure and cannot see why they should not get help from the massed ranks of the department. There is usually nothing for it but to stick to your guns. You must certainly never ever start writing political speeches. But holding the line is much easier if you have first established yourself as someone who is keen and highly able to help Ministers achieve their objectives.

The Number 10 Policy Unit contains a mixture of Special Advisers and permanent civil servants. Individuals within the unit can be very influential. You should therefore work closely with the member of the unit assigned to shadow your department, whenever your subject comes to their attention. Equally, however, don't automatically assume that any one individual in the unit is speaking on behalf of the unit, or on behalf of the Prime Minister. They may well be doing so, but they may also be giving their own views which may not be shared by others.

Parliamentary Clerks look after departments' relations with Parliament, ensuring that questions are answered, Bill amendments laid and so on. They are usually both very knowledgeable and helpful. Indeed, they like to be asked questions because it greatly helps them if you understand their systems and timescales.

Information Officers work in the Press Office but usually develop a very close working relationship with Ministers, and so should form a key part of your extended team. They will help you design media strategies, draft press releases etc. and they will oversee any contact with journalists. Involve them very early on, as you need to 'design in' the way in which you will explain and communicate any new policy. However, like you, they will not seek to 'spin' a story in the sense of seeking to leave a journalist with an over-favourable impression of a development. New Ministers and Special Advisers therefore frequently compare them unfavourably with Party press officers, although the more experienced ones come to admire the trust that can be built up between specialist reporters and their departmental opposite numbers.

Ministers' Duties

Ministers owe certain important duties to their civil servants.

First, they must consider your advice, even if they do not take it. They cannot tell you what to do without first giving you an opportunity to advise them on the suitability of their proposed course of action. The Ministerial Code says that 'Ministers have a duty to give fair consideration and due weight to informed and impartial advice from civil servants . . . '.

On the other hand, Ministers are, to some extent, free to choose how they will receive your advice. Some will have meetings only with selected officials. If you are not in that group then you will always have to submit advice on paper. Other Ministers hate paper, and you will need to be able to brief them – succinctly but effectively – in meetings or in the back of the Ministerial car. But note that Ministers may not require you to give them advice in a public forum, and the advice that you give to Ministers will not normally be made public. It can be difficult enough to give contentious advice whilst worrying about the reactions of your colleagues. It is twice as difficult if you also have to take account of the possible reaction of outside observers, journalists or television viewers. Equally, it is important that Ministers should be allowed to reject your advice without fearing criticism for having done so.

But note also that, if the decision is important, you must prepare, and the Minister must accept, a written submission. Important decisions must never be based merely on oral briefing, or a PowerPoint presentation. This is mainly to ensure that the decision is soundly based on a proper consideration of all the relevant facts and arguments. For instance, a Minister, pleased with the apparent success of a programme, might encourage his or her officials to think about an encore. Such encouragement can sometimes appear welcome, but must be resisted until the case for and against the further programme has been properly thought through. And there is a less positive reason. A formal submission is a defence against a Minister who might not accept advice and then subsequently seeks to blame his or her officials.

If a Minister makes a decision that you consider to be seriously wrong then you have the right – indeed it is your responsibility – to check (a) that the Minister has been presented in writing with all the relevant facts and arguments, and with a clear recommendation, in a form which he can easily assimilate, and (b) that he or she has understood all the important factors. If this has not happened then you should consult the Minister's Private Secretary about the best way to correct matters.

Further written advice will often be enough, including any necessary apology for failing to prepare comprehensive advice the first time round. But if comprehensive advice has already been submitted, and the decision is important enough, then you are entitled to argue the case a second time, preferably in person. If the Minister then still rejects your recommendation then you must accept the decision. It is not for you to question the political or strategic thinking that might have contributed to the decision in question unless, exceptionally, the Minister appears to be ignoring legal advice or defying Government policy, e.g. by failing to consult interested colleagues.

Second, Ministers may not ask you to help them circumvent

collective discussion, e.g. by announcing a 'decision' whilst a Ministerial colleague remains opposed to it. If you are caught in such cross fire you should either refer the issue to your Permanent Secretary or seek collective resolution by involving the Cabinet Secretariat who will arrange discussions at the necessary level.

Third, Ministers may not ask you to do things which are illegal or improper. For instance, they may not ask you to pay a 'state aid' which is prohibited under European Law. And they may not tell you to commit expenditure unless you have obtained the necessary approvals, e.g. from the Treasury. (It is not enough for your Minister to assure you that he has spoken to the Chief Secretary and received the OK. The Chief Secretary may have a quite different recollection of the same conversation, or at the very least has a duty to consult his or her civil servants before making the decision.)

Fourth, Ministers may not ask you to hide things from interested officials and Ministers in your own or other departments. It is of course sometimes sensible to work up a proposal before showing it to colleagues. After all, although you do not work only for your own Ministers, you certainly work first for your Ministers. But you may not collude in a 'bounce' and if you feel that colleagues in another department would expect to be told about a proposal, then you must tell them – and you should ensure that your Ministers are equally well informed. It is embarrassing, to say the least, if they find that the Chief Secretary appears to know more than they do.

The main exception to this rule is that there is no need for you to disclose your own and your Minister's negotiating position in a public expenditure negotiation. But the relevant facts which underlie your position must be disclosed.

Fifth, Ministers should be polite to their officials – because of course we cannot answer back. In practice, we can forgive an occasional flash of bad temper, recognising that Ministers are often under great pressure. Indeed, it is worth remembering that Ministers who are constantly charming in public may sometimes be less than charming to their staff (and vice versa). I suspect that that is because we all have only a limited amount of charm to hand around. And Ministers are human, too, with the usual run of human strengths and weaknesses. But consistent bullying, rudeness and foul language are unacceptable.

It can be hard to know what to do if a Minister appears to be breaking one of the above rules. If you know the Minister well enough, and if you are sure that you are not being thin skinned, you should raise any concerns yourself. Alternatively you might consult the Minister's Private Secretary. And failing that you should enlist the help of a senior colleague.

Giving Advice to Ministers

We have a professional duty to give clear unbiased advice, based on a sound knowledge of the facts and a wise analysis of the competing arguments. Above all, we understand the need to question both explicit and implicit assumptions, especially those about human, corporate or national economic behaviour. We make full use of our common sense or instincts, drawing on our experience in the policy area in question. And we above all give advice which will deliver worthwhile outcomes, not just in some idealised Whitehall world but in real schools, hospitals, or barracks.

The best civil servants are also very good at putting themselves in Ministers' shoes, and understanding their fears, ambitions and pressures. We understand that Ministers are on the shortest of short term contracts and are constantly trying to balance a number of conflicting pressures. Ministers need to know that civil servants understand those pressures. If this does not come naturally, then set some time aside to reflect on why Ministers took that unexpected decision, or said or wrote that unexpected thing. There is always a reason, even if you would not always agree that it is a good one.

The best civil servants also know that their advice will often be unwelcome or unexpected, so they do not expect it to be accepted straight away. There is usually a moment to be seized, but you might have to wait for it.

Indeed, you should never tell a Minister that he or she cannot do something unless you also offer them an alternative approach which substantially achieves the same political objective, or at the very least undertake to look for a way round the obstacle, and to report back very quickly. You must therefore develop the ability to distinguish between Ministers' fundamental objectives and the specific solutions which they might put forward, but which might not be workable or affordable.

Remember, too, that, as Ministers are under constant pressure, you must do everything possible to help them work quickly, efficiently and effectively. Always prepare your work in a way which allows them to concentrate on essential decisions, and on presentation. Be succinct – especially in meetings.

Ministers are inevitably very concerned to perform well in Parliament. It is particularly important that they are well prepared for Oral Parliamentary Questions, Statements and Debates, all of which can be very testing even for experienced Ministers. On the other hand, do not make the mistake of believing that political opponents are also enemies. Parliament operates rather like an old-fashioned club. Fierce public debate is often for show, and political opponents are often surprisingly friendly when not on public view.

Ministers hate it when civil servants hog the thinking time. It is often the case that we know that a difficult decision needs to be taken in, for example, five days time. We then spend four (or four-

and-a-half) days crafting elegant advice. This cannot possibly allow the Minister enough time to reflect on the issue, let alone ask for further information or consultations. Of course it will take you some time to consult colleagues, consider all the options etc. But, as a rule of thumb, you should put up a preliminary submission, if only for information, about half way through your thinking period. If nothing else, this will give the Minister a chance to reflect on the issue in bed at night. And he or she will be able to feed in their own thoughts and questions, before it is too late. We may not welcome substantial changes to our proposals – but it is better to know about them before the deadline is only a few hours away.

Similarly, Ministers hate surprises. They need to be told bad news, told about serious problems, and told when important decisions are brewing, as soon as you are aware of them. They may not be very pleased, but they will be a lot less pleased if they first hear of the problem from someone else, or even worse from the press, and then find out that you knew all along.

There is of course a lot more to persuading a Minister than simply providing logical advice. As noted above, your advice is much more likely to be accepted if you have already established that you under-stand political realities. You also need to show that you can cope with setbacks and can dig yourself – and your Minister – out of a hole. Indeed, if you have made a mistake yourself, and then said 'sorry' and done your best to put it right, you will probably find that this results in your having a stronger relationship with your Minister. He or she will have made mistakes too!

More widely, however, you need to show that you understand 'the real world' outside Whitehall, and are innovative and enthusiastic. I will return to understanding the real world, and innovation, later in this book. As for the need for enthusiasm, you need to remember that personal impressions count heavily with Ministers. They want to be able to rely on their officials, and are very disappointed if officials do not seem committed to their objectives and are in any way unimpressive, hesitant or over-cautious; or if they do not seem to know what they are talking about. You are paid to be creative and to look for solutions. You should make it clear that obstacles frustrate you, too. You should also tell them about your successes, and prepare very carefully for even the most routine meetings with them. This will reinforce their trust in you, and this in turn will give you greater authority in your dealings with others.

Also (I hate to say this, but it is important) remember that your clothes, appearance and body language send clear messages, whether or not you want them to. Take care that those messages are the ones that you wish to send, both to Ministers and to colleagues.

Civil Servants

Now let's have a look at your fellow civil servants.

When you arrive on your first day, you will first meet support staff (or 'administrative staff') in reception areas, delivering papers, and so on. They also carry out routine casework and provide direct support for senior staff. They are very important, not only because nothing would function without them, but also because they see more clearly than anyone else what is going on. If you want to know whether a unit is well run, and provides a good service to its customers, you will get a better informed, and more honest, answer from support staff.

Next up the chain are middle management (or 'executive grades'). They help formulate and amend policy; deal with more difficult casework and help Ministers respond to letters from the public. A small number of them are in the 'fast stream' – serving a three to five year apprenticeship before being promoted to Grade 7 and then into the Senior Civil Service.

Titles such as 'Grade 7', or the even older 'Principal', are old-fashioned, and have been superseded by a wide range of other titles. Grade 7 has become Range 10, Band A, Deputy Director, Assistant Director, and Range E, to name but five. But there is no common title used across Whitehall, so the old titles live on, including in this

Table 1

	Very Old Title	Old Title	Nowadays often known as
Senior Civil Service	Head of the Civil Service		
	Permanent Secretary (Civil Service head of each department)		
	Deputy Secretary	Grade 2	Director General
	Under Secretary	Grade 3	Director
	Assistant Secretary	Grade 5	Director or Deputy Director
	Senior Principal and Principal	Grade 6 and Grade 7	Deputy Director, Assistant Director, Team Leader, Policy Manager etc.

book. The main ones, at Grade 7 and above, are shown in table 1 What do these senior people do? They help Ministers and other officials deliver Ministers' objectives, both by giving advice to Ministers and by implementing Ministers' decisions. They need to be able to work closely and effectively with Ministers, with other Whitehall civil servants, with the wider civil service, with the private and voluntary sectors and with pressure groups. They operate more like a club than a hierarchical organisation – and that is simultaneously their great strength and their great weakness – a subject to which I return later.

The key grade is Grade 7. Grade 7s are expected to know all there is to know about their policy area, and to know all the key players, pressure groups and so on. In a well-run department, you will find that senior officials listen very carefully to their Grade 7s, and tend to operate in a way which supports their Grade 7s, rather than vice versa.

There are around 3700 people in the Senior Civil Service (SCS), including many outside Whitehall, many specialists and many who first worked in other sectors. Indeed, the long term aim is to have around one-third of the SCS recruited from outside the civil service. SCS jobs vary hugely, but usually include one or more of the following:

- agreeing strategic aims with Ministers, and communicating those aims to Grade 7s and others;
- agreeing and providing the financial and human resources needed to achieve those aims;
- deploying their greater knowledge and experience in support of Grade 7s;
- trouble-shooting;
- undertaking complex casework and project management;
- acting as a personal adviser to Ministers, of whom more below.

The breadth of responsibilities increases with increasing grade, but it is seldom necessary for there to be a Grade 5 and a Grade 3 and a Grade 2 between the key Grade 7 and the Permanent Secretary/Head of Department. Most departments structure themselves so as to cut out one of these tiers (but not always the same one) in each management hierarchy.

It is worth noting that the more senior officials are not necessarily more powerful. They have to rely on others both for information and for delivery, and they are often heavily constrained by (small p) political factors, including the independence of each Secretary of

State, and hence the independence of each departmental senior management team. Other constraints on senior officials include the need to avoid annoying Ministers, and the club-like nature of senior officialdom. The latter can be a good thing, in that it encourages senior officials to work collaboratively rather than just for their own Ministers. It also allows pay levels to be set relatively low, in return for lots of genuine job satisfaction.(The median total Grade 3 remuneration package, for instance, was in 1999 worth only 40 per cent of that of private sector comparators). But the 'clubiness' of the Senior Civil Service can also lead to senior officials being over-tactful in their dealings with one another, which can delay change and create confused expectations.

2   Professional Skills

Effective Communication

Both Ministers and officials live or die by our communications skills. We often have no other weapon at our disposal. But we are not communicating with machines. We are trying to achieve things by influencing the behaviour of other human beings. Whether written or oral, our communications need to be alive, and for this purpose they need emotion, they need energy and they need intelligence. They also need to be planned.

Emotion
We should never neglect the need for emotion and humanity when we speak and when we write, either for our own or for Minister's signature. Emotions make a very clear impression on those with whom we are communicating, and contribute greatly to the effectiveness of our communications. They should therefore form a small but vital part of almost all communications, including inter-Ministerial correspondence, Ministerial submissions, letters to the public and speeches – indeed any communication in which you are trying to persuade or leave a lasting impression. Dry, official sounding texts are simply less effective in these circumstances.

We must also always be polite and, if there is anything to apologise for – including a late reply – then apologise generously, using the word 'sorry' (as ever, a short Anglo-Saxon word is the most effective). Always try to avoid jargon, officialese, legalese, foreign or

Latin phrases, acronyms and abbreviations. And please avoid insincerity. I distrust rounding off sentences at the end of letters e.g. 'I hope you find these comments helpful'. These words are certainly entirely inappropriate if the letter conveys unwelcome news.

Energy

To be effective it is also necessary to impart some sense of motivation, commitment or direction. For instance, it is not enough to demonstrate, in a Ministerial submission, that you are familiar with the facts, and are concerned about them. You also have to show that you intend to do something about the issue. Only then will a Minister be happy to leave you to get on with your job.

Similarly, a Minister, when writing to colleagues or the public, needs to demonstrate that he or she appreciates what is troubling the correspondent and, demonstrate his or her determination to deal with the point at issue.

After you have drafted a letter, take a good look at it to make sure that it passes the above tests.

Intelligence

Your approach to the draft will depend, of course, on whether you are still at the stage of designing your policy, or whether you are implementing or defending it. But, whichever applies, it is essential that the contents are logical and accurate, whether we are communicating within Whitehall or with the public. Many of our communications deal with subjects which are important either to our Ministers or to sections of the public, or to both. None of us will get very far unless we learn to write accurately and unambiguously, and indeed all experienced civil servants have real skill in this area. It is also essential that we properly explain the considerations which underlie Minister's policies. It is a real cop out to use phrases such as 'It is the department's policy that . . . '. The obvious retort is 'Why?'.

The structure of written text can make all the difference, especially if the subject is a complex one. Do not hesitate to make full use of side headings. 'Background' and 'Next Steps' or 'Action' are particularly useful. Also make full use of annexes to reduce the length, and improve the flow, of the main document. If you are asking more than one question, or dealing with more than one issue, consider giving each a separate section and a separate heading. And remember that one table of figures, or one graph, can often do the job of several pages of words.

We sometimes have to deal with people who are highly stressed or obsessive or worse. Such people need to receive very clear unambiguous information and advice, or else you will get absolutely nowhere. It is always a mistake to be rude or to show anger or frustration. Such reactions (a) raise the emotional temperature, and so get in the way of clear communication; (b) immediately make people dislike you, and (c) lay you open to criticism. All these severely reduce your effectiveness.

Planning

Before you turn to your keyboard, dictaphone or pen, or turn up for a meeting, take a little time to decide:

- what you expect to the recipient to do once they have read your missive, or what action you expect to be taken following your meeting
- when you expect it to be done, and (if appropriate)
- how much work you expect to create.

The answers to these questions are not always obvious and, if they are not obvious to you, they will certainly not be obvious to the recipient. It is particularly important to think about the amount of work that you are creating. You may think you are asking a simple question, but the recipient might be able to answer it at a number of levels after varying degrees of research. So do you want them to spend 15 minutes, or 15 hours, on the reply?

The question is particularly relevant if you are addressing a request to several people. For instance, if you send out a request for briefing or information to the Heads of only 10 Divisions, but they each pass it out to four Branches, and if each Branch then has to do three hours work, you have created 120 hours of work. Even more work can be created by Ministerial correspondence and letters to trade associations and the heads of large companies. Do you really intend this? Could you not target the request more carefully, or write to a sample of recipients?

Once you have answered the above three questions to your own satisfaction, you should include the result in the first few sentences of your letter or minute, or at the end of the meeting. There is no need for this to appear as an order. You can add plenty of words and phrases like 'please', 'I should be grateful if' and 'it would be helpful if'. But do not disguise your expectations. The recipient needs these to be crystal clear.

If you are simply seeking agreement to a proposal, phrase your minute in such a way that a simple 'yes' or 'no' can be given by the recipient, e.g. finish the minute: 'Do you agree please?'.

Presentation

I make no apology for stressing the importance of presentation so early in this book. It is an intrinsic part of policy development, because it is never enough, in today's society, merely to introduce new laws and regulations and then expect instant obedience. We have to get the population on our side, or else even the cleverest of policies will fail. Indeed, some parts of Whitehall have come to recognise that they are involved in what amounts to a permanent campaign.

You must also remember that very few people read guidance material, however well written. New regulations therefore need to be easy to understand, and clearly communicated via the media, if they are to be generally accepted and easily enforced. The main purpose of guidance material should be to answer questions about the application of the new rules to non-standard situations.

We must therefore design policies that are easily communicated. Furthermore, presentation needs to be considered right at the beginning of the policy process, not near the end, for policies that are hard to understand, and hard to defend, are generally flawed. The time to think about this is before you choose your policy option, not right at the end of the process. White Papers, consultation documents etc. should make it crystal clear how each proposal will make life better for ordinary members of the public, for business or for other sectors.

Let's now fast forward beyond the policy design stage to the point at which Ministers' decisions need to be announced, and so become the object of critical scrutiny by other politicians and the media. We now have a duty to be less analytical and help Ministers present their policies and decisions in the best possible light. In order to carry out this task, we must put aside any doubts (and sometimes also put aside inconvenient facts) and look at the issue through Ministers' eyes in order to help them express their beliefs and defend their policies as effectively as possible.

Whenever you are thinking about the presentational aspects of a policy, are some things to bear in mind.

- First, we need to be constantly on the look out for opportunities for Ministers to publicise their policies and their programmes.

We need to be pro-active in looking for media and other opportunities, including in connection with developments in related policy areas elsewhere in the department or Whitehall.

- Second, don't be mesmerised by the media. There are lots of other ways to communicate your policies, including via the web and by getting key opinion formers and senior stakeholders on your side.

- Third, Ministers will usually want their policies to be set within the Government's wider agenda. So every important speech, letter or magazine article has to speak to current key themes before focusing down on its particular subject. If you do not have a note of current themes – and they do change from time to time – then consult your Press Office.

- Fourth, do bear in mind that there are strict limits to how far we can go without compromising our political impartiality. On the one hand, it is perfectly proper for us to prepare drafts for Ministers (including draft Parliamentary Answers) which praise the Government's policies, and it is perfectly proper for our drafts to omit facts and arguments which might cast doubt on the appropriateness of those policies. In doing this, we are not being unprofessional. Rather, like the barrister whose principal duty is to the court and who does not necessarily believe in the client's case, we are simply providing the best possible professional service to our clients, without going so far as to mislead either the Minister or Parliament. On the other hand, we may not explicitly or implicitly criticise members of, nor the policies of, the Opposition, nor may we criticise the actions or performance of the current Opposition whilst they were in Government. Also, anything in a draft that purports to be a fact must be verifiable. Nor may we serve up unverifiable generalisations. If you feel that Ministers would want to make a statement which cannot be verified then you should suggest that they say something like: 'I believe it is clear that . . .' or something of the sort, so attributing the statement to the Minister, rather than implying that it cannot be questioned.

Incidentally, Ministers are particularly sensitive about publications put out by departments. Even the most obscure of documents can contain embarrassing 'expert's' comments or ambiguous facts – often stuck in an obscure annex. Commentators will then use the document to attack a Minister – even though he or she may never have seen it. Of course such documents must still be published, but Ministers are entitled to be warned about possible problems, and given an opportunity to prepare their comments. All documents should therefore be read in detail by someone other than their author to check for problems.

And you should be particularly careful when supporting your Minister in 'the box' in the House of Commons, or sitting in a Committee room anywhere in Parliament. In particular, it is a dead give away if you put your head in your hands when your Minister is asked the one question that you have particularly dreaded!

Submissions

Your formal advice to Ministers, or requests for approvals and authorisations, will be contained in a written submission. Emails, PowerPoint presentations and conversations are excellent ways of taking discussions forward but they should never be used for important decisions.

Each department has its own preferred submission structure, but a very good one, used by a number of departments, is: *Issue, Recommendation, Timing, Background, Argument, Presentation.* If the issue is a simple one, you can condense the issue, recommendation and timing into one paragraph, but the other items should always be kept separate, even if each is quite short.

The advantage of this structure is that it brings the Recommendations and Timing sections to the early attention of the Minister, so that they can be borne in mind whilst the rest of the submission is being digested, or even ignored if the recommendation is clearly attractive (or unavoidable). But some Ministers prefer always to read the supporting detail, and their wishes should be respected, even if the result is that they ask that their submissions are structured in a different way. It is vital that Ministers should be given the facts and arguments that they believe necessary so that they can take good decisions in which they have real confidence.

Before starting to draft, consider carefully whether you are seeking to formulate policy; or helping promote, defend or implement it. The tone, substance and length of your submission will be greatly affected by this decision. It can then be helpful to prepare a first draft of the submission in the following order:

- *Presentation*: First, you should if possible draft the press notice which will communicate the decision that you are recommending. It may be too soon to show your draft to a Minister but, if the draft comes easily, then the rest of the submission will probably flow quite naturally. On the other hand, policies that are hard to understand, and hard to defend, are often flawed. Deal also with other presentational issues, such as the method of any announcement, media handling, and so on.
- *The Issue*: a brief statement of the problem or the decision that needs to be taken.
- *Background*: provide sufficient facts and a summary of the story so far, including a rehearsal of previous Ministerial decisions and

correspondence. If referring to documents, summarise or attach them. But consider how much the Minister already knows or will remember, for it is often possible to reduce the background to a couple of sentences.

- *Argument*: the considerations, based on the (above) background, which lead you to clearly identified conclusions and recommendations. Summarise all the reasonably possible options and deal (perhaps briefly) with the merits and demerits of each one.

- *Recommendations*: Now summarise your conclusions and recommendations, cross-referenced to the appropriate paragraphs of the argument section. If possible, you should phrase your advice so that the Minister can just say 'yes' or 'no'. Do not merely recommend a discussion with officials. It is important that you should recommend a specific course of action or decision, taking into account Ministers' declared policies and political agenda. If Ministers accept your recommendation then you have saved yourself and them a meeting. If not, any discussion will be assisted by the Minister having a firm recommendation to discuss and test.

- *Timing*: a note of the time scale within which the decision needs to be taken, with an explanation if there is a need for urgency.

The final draft can then if necessary be re-ordered to bring the Recommendations and Timing sections up front. It can also be shortened! Because Ministers are under constant pressure, you should be as succinct as possible. If you really cannot bear to cut stuff out, then at least consider putting it in an annex. It may never get read but it might make you feel better.

Incidentally, try not to take yourself or your advice too seriously. You may well analyse a problem in great depth and craft an elegant submission which convinces you and everyone around you of the merits of your recommendation. But issues are seldom really black and white, and the world will not come to an end if the Minister disagrees with you. And even if your advice is not accepted, its preparation will certainly not have been a waste of time, for it will have prepared the Minister for attacks from any commentators and political opponents who independently come up with the same conclusion as you.

Briefing

If a Minister is about to hold a meeting, take part in a discussion, or make an official visit, you will submit written briefing. It is easy to forget that the primary purpose of a written briefing is to help Ministers achieve their objectives for the meeting. In order for this to happen all briefings should include the following elements, preferably in this order.

- *Reason For The Meeting*: Provide a brief explanation of why the meeting, visit etc. was arranged and who asked for it, e.g. 'You asked us to arrange this meeting to try to resolve the disagreement between . . . ' or 'This is another in the series of meetings in which you are meeting children's charities.'
- *Directions, Agenda etc:* These are very important! The person being briefed (or their Private Secretary) has to know when the meeting is taking place, how to get to it and what is to be discussed. The agenda should be agreed in advance with other participants and should, in the case of a long meeting, suggest starting times for each item.
- *Objectives:* This is the most important part of the brief. You must clearly identify what needs to be achieved if the meeting or visit is to be judged a success, e.g. 'The objective is to get the organisation to agree that . . . ' or 'The objective is to agree a price of £10m or

less, for [the project] completed by the end of October', or 'Your objective is to learn about the company and the industry. But the company should also be given an opportunity to lobby about its current planning difficulties (see letter of . . . at Annex . . .)'.

Above all, as ever, think very carefully about whether the meeting is intended to help the Minister decide his/her policy direction – in which case he or she can be encouraged to enter into a fairly open discussion – or whether the meeting is intended to help the Minister achieve his or her pre-determined objectives, in which case his or her style will need to be more proactive or defensive as the case might be. Meetings with other Ministers should generally fall into the first category. It is a great mistake to encourage Ministers to take fixed positions when discussing genuinely difficult issues with colleagues – if only because the other Ministers will respond by adopting fixed positions themselves, so everybody wastes time.

- *Line to Take:* This is the section that the Minister will have in front of him at a formal meeting. Consider repeating it on a card, printed in large type in 1.5 spacing. Provide key points that need to be made and then, if necessary, add defensive material such as areas of vulnerability and the counter arguments. The whole thing should be in a form that can be read out. Do not include confidential material here, in case it too is read out!
- *Participants:* You should provide the forenames and surnames, and positions, of the principal people who will be at the meeting or the principal hosts of a visit. And unless the person being briefed knows them quite well, add a brief c.v. and a note of other important or other relevant facts.
- *Background:* This is often the least important part of the briefing. In general, the length of the background should be in proportion

to the length, complexity and importance of the meeting, and in inverse proportion to the knowledge of the person being briefed. A first, day-long visit to a major institution will therefore justify comprehensive background briefing, including a copy of their latest annual report. You may also consider using a commercial database or the internet. And briefing for a difficult or complex negotiation must include a summary of previous discussions (whether at official or Ministerial level) as well as copies of all documents, legislation etc. that might be referred to. On the other hand a second or third, essentially courtesy call might require little more background briefing than a reference to recent news, or recently-raised issues.

Finally, try to ensure that one official takes responsibility for gathering together, and clearly presenting, all the briefing for a meeting, even if several officials provide contributions. It may seem to officials that the meeting will deal with a number of different subjects, but the Minister will see only one meeting and needs to be presented with one set of objectives, one agenda and one set of papers, clearly presented and flagged.

Ministerial Correspondence

You will draft replies to a huge number of letters during your career, both for your own signature and that of others. The key thing to remember is that you should draft a letter which:

- positively, persuasively, clearly and accurately states the Minister's views
- clearly sets out any follow up action, and
- provides a full reply to the incoming correspondence.

Letters should also:

- show that the Minister appreciates what is troubling the correspondent,
- be polite and helpful
- use clear, uncomplicated language and short sentences, and
- be to the point, avoiding jargon and references to legislation unless they are absolutely necessary

As always, you must be clear, before you start on the reply, what mode you are in. Is the correspondence part of the process through which policy is decided, or are you are in 'promote/defend' or 'implement' mode? Correspondence about policy development or policy implementation can be more interesting, because you can (or the Minster can) admit uncertainty and enter into genuine debate. Defensive letters are more boring, because you want to close the correspondence. It is therefore tempting – and sometimes necessary – to draft something very short, simply saying that the correspondent's views have been noted, or rehearsing the Government's position without responding to the particular points in the incoming letter. But try to do better than this. The person at the other end will almost certainly have invested a lot of time and emotion in the letter to the Minister and it is awful if they just get a brush off by way of reply. Equally, however, do not beat about the bush if, for instance, there is little or no prospect of the Minister agreeing to something, including an invitation.

Now a word about mechanics. Private Offices divide incoming correspondence into four broad categories.

First, there is inter-Ministerial correspondence – formal letters or minutes sent from a Minister in one department to a colleague in another. These are very important bits of paper because they represent the main route through which policy problems are aired and resolved. An odd feature is the copy list which is in the final paragraph 'I am copying this letter to the Prime Minister, the Chancellor of the Exchequer . . . and to Sir Humphrey Appleby [i.e. to the Cabinet Secretariat]'. When drafting the reply you should never say 'I am copying this letter to recipients of yours' – for this makes life very difficult for Private Office correspondence clerks who will not have the original letter easily to hand.

Next, there are letters and emails to which the Minister will reply. These include most letters from MPs, MEPs, members of the devolved administrations and key opinion-formers. You will in time become quite expert at drafting replies to such letters. Replies to MP's letters usually begin:

> *Thank you for your letter of [date] enclosing correspondence*
> *from your constituent, Mrs . . . , [Managing Director of . . .*
> *Co Ltd.] of [full address] about [subject].*

The third category – relatively small in number – consists of MPs' and similar letters which are passed on to senior civil servants, usually Agency Chief Executives, for them to reply in their own name. This happens only when the result is that the correspondence is handled in a way most likely to meet the needs of the MP and his or her constituent. The usual benefits are that the MP and his or her constituent get a quicker reply; the reply comes from the person who has direct responsibility for the subject matter of the correspondence, and direct access to the facts; and there are paper handling and staff cost savings. However, if an MP specifically asks for a Ministerial reply, then this must be given. And officials should never reply to MPs' or similar correspondence which raises political issues, or issues on which the policy is not settled.

Then comes the largest category of all, the letters from the public which are sent down for 'official reply'. These vary hugely in style, content and importance. It is therefore a great mistake to treat them all in the same way. Some will be so interesting or important that the Minister should be asked to reply. And others will not need a reply at all. But the majority will receive a reply, which might begin:

> *Thank you for your letter of [date] to the Secretary of State for . . . about [subject]. I have been asked to reply.*

You will become particularly adept at drafting polite replies to the numerous invitations that reach Ministers' offices. Indeed, it can be particularly tricky to draft a reply to an invitation. Some suggestions, to get you started, are in Annex 1 at the end of this book.

Incidentally, it is useful to know that:

- Those honoured by the Queen become 'Sirs', 'OBEs' etc. on the day of announcement. But it takes two or three weeks before a new Lord or Baroness is properly created. Until then they retain their former status.
- Only Privy Counsellors (i.e. all current and former Cabinet Ministers and a few current or former senior non-Cabinet Ministers) are 'Rt. Hon.'.
- It is best to refer to Baronesses as 'Baroness X' rather than 'Lady X', so as to distinguish them from women who become 'Ladies' when their husbands become 'Sirs'.

Speeches

I guess that most people are born able to write a good speech, just as they can learn any language. Unfortunately, the ability is usually knocked out of us as we become self-conscious, and over-dominated by the written word. The following tips are intended to help those who wish to re-learn the ability to write an interesting speech, whether for a Minister, a colleague or themselves.

To begin with, you must first be absolutely clear whether the speech needs to be delivered in the first place. Speeches are very time-consuming, both in their preparation and in the travel time to and from the venue. Remember that Ministerial speeches need to tread a fine line between being dull and dangerous. Are you sure that the Minister will have something interesting and/or original to say, and will not be unnecessarily controversial? If so, is the audience the right one? Will there be an opportunity for publicity?

Unfortunately, all too many invitations are from organisations that need to fill an after dinner slot or something of the sort. The last thing they want is a thoughtful speech about the weighty issue of the day – especially if the content might be critical of the community to which the audience belongs. Let's face it: half the audience will be tipsy – or worse – and the majority will certainly want to be entertained. Leave these challenges to professional after dinner speakers. And if the Minister wants to appear for political reasons, or to raise his or her profile, then let the Special Adviser write the speech. He or she will know more jokes than you do.

But of course a properly prepared speech, delivered at the right time to the right audience, can be highly effective. As ever, planning and preparation are the key.

First, remember your three duties and decide which you are carrying out when drafting the speech. Is the Minister going to talk fairly freely about possible policy developments? Or are you helping to promote or defend Ministers' policies in which case a more barn-storming approach will be needed. Or maybe you are even in implementation mode, which would require a quite different approach again. But do bear in mind that many audiences object to simply hearing the party line. A more considered, thoughtful and consultative speech will generally go down much better.

Second, you also need to identify those one or two key messages that you and/or the speaker want to leave in the minds of the audience. What do you want them to do differently after hearing the speech? What do you want them to remember some days afterwards?

Third, you should also find out what the audience wants to get out of the speech. The easiest way to do this is to ask the event organiser what will go down well, what information needs to be put over and what will please the audience. Your one – or at the most two – key messages can then be nicely wrapped so that the audience is first made receptive to the key messages – especially if they are likely to be unwelcome or surprising.

Take particular care correctly to define and describe the nature of the speech. A 'keynote address' should include the key points which will be the main topics for discussion for the rest of the conference. An 'opening address' will set the scene or set out the Government's position as a prelude to more detailed speeches. In this case you should take care that the Minister's comments will not duplicate any other opening remarks by the Chair or host.

When you have decided what you want to say, then plan your structure. You can do much worse than stick to the traditional:

- tell them what your main message will be, then,
- deliver the message, and then,
- tell them what the message was!

There may be other ways of structuring a speech, but no other way works every time, or leaves such a clear impression.

Drafting

Actually, the worst thing you can do is either 'draft' or 'write' a speech. If a speech reads well, especially to colleagues, it will sound stilted and boring. You should simply pick up a dictaphone, put your speech structure on the table in front of you, and start talking. If you get stuck, think about the audience and talk about them and the issues that face them. Use plenty of anecdotes and illustrations, avoid long lists and let detailed statistics give way to easily grasped facts (e.g. 'last year we doubled our exports to X' rather than 'in 2004 our exports to X were 92 per cent up on 2003'). Above all, get some emotion into it, and some power. The result will be much more interesting – and more natural.

Then check the typed text for unclear or misleading phrases, remove platitudes and generalities, and check that it consists only of sentences which are less than two lines long. Finally, read the whole thing through out loud, to make sure that it trips off the tongue fairly easily. Do not, as has happened, ask a Minister to describe how he has 'instituted an epidemiological survey'.

You will of course need to show the draft to colleagues affected by its content. But unless it contains a major statement of Government policy, try to avoid showing it to senior colleagues. They will only start fretting about the colloquial language and the split infinitives, and turn the whole thing into an essay which will read well, but sound awful.

On the day always check the technology. Is the speaker familiar with the microphone and/or teleprompter, and does it work? Ditto the projector and/or video player. Does he or she know how to control them?

It is also worth listening carefully to the speech, even if you know every word off by heart. Try to tune into the Minister's speech patterns, sense of timing etc. You will never mimic them exactly, but it will help you when you next settle down to dictate a speech.

And afterwards check how the speech was received. If it went down badly, you can blame the speaker. Either way, you will learn something for the future. But don't fret if the speech really bombed. It happens to us all.

Lobbies and Lobbyists

You will meet a lot of people who are trying to get the Government to act in a way which will be to their advantage. A small number will lobby on behalf of others – and especially on behalf of those who cannot lobby for themselves. And occasionally – but probably not very often – you will come across a professional lobbyist working on behalf of a client.

The key thing to remember is that, in one respect, they all want the same thing – which is for their message to be understood. They will therefore react very badly, and pester you much more, if they think that you are being over-defensive, or cannot be bothered with them, or that they are being fobbed off. So always put yourself in their shoes, emphasise that you do understand their concern, and that their views will genuinely be taken into account.

Campaign letters – hundreds or thousands of them – can be a logistical nightmare. You first need to decide whether they need a response. It is better, of course, if you can reply to each one, especially in view of the principle outlined above. But individual responses are usually out of the question. Maybe you can send a really well-written response to the organisation that has organised the campaign, and they can distribute it in their newsletter? Or even better, these days, you might use the internet.

Serious lobbyists will ask for a meeting and you should generally agree to such requests, partly to show that you have not closed your mind, and partly because a good discussion can often lead to surprising insights which might help you crack the underlying problem. And don't get upset if they ask to see 'someone senior' or a Minister. After all, they want to know that their message is getting beyond you, and how better than to deliver it in person? If the person lobbying is sufficiently senior, or the campaign is high profile, then you should ensure that they are seen at an appropriately high level. The exact level is always a question of fine judgement, but the aim, as always, should be to reassure the caller that the department and its Minister are taking them seriously. If that needs a Minister, then so be it. Equally, however, I have often pointed out to lobbyists that they will only get a few minutes of a Minister's time, or of the time of a senior official, whereas they could spend much longer, and have a more fruitful dialogue, with the departmental expert.

Status can be a problem the other way round. Some large companies have middle or senior managers who lobby hard in support of their particular responsibility. A research director, for instance, might press you to spend huge sums supporting research & development in their area, whilst a property manager might want you to relax planning laws. It is always worth checking that they have the full support of their own senior colleagues. For instance, does their chairman, who so often rails against excessive Government expenditure, really support the proposed £100m Government research programme? Or does he really want rid of green belt controls, bearing in mind his vehement opposition to the expansion of a computer laboratory in his pleasant Cambridgeshire village? If so, let him come in and tell Ministers to their faces. Such meetings add small pleasures to otherwise dull days.

You need to be more tough with those who ask for repeat meetings when they have very little new to say. Consider carefully whether you have done enough to keep them in touch with developments. If so, then you may simply have to refuse a meeting which is going to be a waste of everyone's time – but maybe soften your refusal with an offer to meet again at a more sensible time.

And watch out that a meeting does not backfire on the lobbyist, particularly when the Minister is acting in a quasi-judicial capacity. For instance, a Minister who agrees to see a party to a planning application may either then have to see all the other parties or decide against the said party in order to avoid being judicially reviewed. It can be amazing how quickly the meeting idea is dropped, once the implications are explained.

Professional lobbyists (and their in-house equivalents, public affairs directors) are generally a good thing, particularly because they ensure that all the arguments are marshalled together and clearly presented. They also provide a helpful service to industrialists and others who are often surprisingly terrified of Whitehall and all the strange beings that stalk its corridors. But they can be very pushy, so you sometimes have to be quite firm in response, especially if they want repeat meetings when there is little more to be said. Luckily they are pretty thick-skinned – and why would you care if they never trouble you again? But take care to ensure that you are not refusing a meeting which might indeed have taken the debate in a useful direction. And make sure you see their client, and not just the lobbyist.

Finally, do not let anyone outside government, however important they are, get the impression that policy is being framed with only their interests in mind. Colleagues elsewhere in government are understandably on the look out for signs of 'departmentalitis' and all too willing to believe that you have 'gone native' and become the unwitting (and unprofessional) advocate for a particular interest. Take care that you frame your arguments in such a way as to make it clear that this is not so.

It follows that you should take particular care to ensure that no-one is allowed to bully either you or a Minister. Conversely, you need to be conscious of the value of the good name of the British Government. The Government sets out to deal fairly and straightforwardly with everyone. In particular, civil servants never bluff. If we say that we will take certain action in certain circumstances then we must mean it. Failure to do so damages the Government's credibility.

Finally, you should never rely on oral representations when important principles, or large amounts of money or careers or reputations, are at stake. Telephone communication is particularly unreliable, for you lose the visual clues that add texture to face-to-face communication. So get everything written down, either in the form of a contract or as your record, copied to the other party, of what they said. For instance, if someone comes in for a meeting (with you or a Minister) as a result of which the Minister might make a controversial decision, ensure that there is an accurate record of what is said, and send it to the person before the decision is made. He or she will not then be able to deny it, or claim that they were misunderstood.

3   The Policy Process

What process? The problem is that new policies, and policy decisions, can arise in, and are handled in, a multitude of different ways, as is made clear by Mark Turner and David Hulme:

> *What must be banished is any lingering idea that policy is some highly rational process in which expert technicians are firmly in control using highly tuned instruments to achieve easily predicted outcomes. Such an image is inappropriate for OECD countries let alone the developing world . . .*

But it is often possible to discern a number of separate stages, including

- identify a problem;
- research;
- consultation and gaining knowledge;
- exploring options;
- more consultation;
- taking a recommendation through to Ministerial agreement.

However, it is important to realise that the individual stages do not operate sequentially, but overlap as policies become firmed up.

To begin at the beginning, someone has to identify a problem or an issue or an opportunity. That 'someone' can include a political party (especially when in opposition and writing a manifesto), a Minister, the media, a pressure group, a think tank, a trade association, an 'expert', a member of the public or a civil servant. The difficulty, therefore, is not that there are too few ideas, but that there are far too many, and it is quite impossible to run with more than a fraction of them. The natural result is that both Ministers and officials are forced to spend much of their time in defensive mode, either explaining why nothing will be done or just avoiding the issue.

Some generators of ideas are more likely than others to be listened to. Ministers, obviously, are in pole position – as long as they concentrate on a small number of initiatives and do not come up with a new idea every day. Outside experts and pressure groups can also be very effective, as long as they are truly respected by their peers. And so can civil servants, but only once they have earned the respect of their Ministers.

So there are some lessons in this for the civil servant. First, try not to be over-defensive. The world is full of good ideas, hidden amongst even more bad ones. Your job is to help Ministers identify the good ones, even if they are counter-intuitive, from an unusual source, or from a highly critical pressure group.

Second, take every opportunity to gain the respect of your Ministers before espousing a novel idea. New Ministers bestow power on those they trust. To begin with, they will prefer to deal with their political advisers and others that have previously supported them through thick and thin. They will come to trust you, as well, and bestow power on you, but only if you earn that trust over a period, and by responding positively to their agenda.

Third, seize an opportunity when it presents itself. Don't let it slip by. The best moments of your career will be when you have put an idea to a Minister, or a Minister has put an idea to you, and you jointly see the possibility of achieving real change. You will dash off to gather colleagues around you, and map out a dramatic and challenging strategy. You will write your ideas up that evening, re-write them when you have calmed down in the morning, and get back to the Minister, with a really positive programme, within 24 hours – and then you really are on your way.

There is a nice example, told by Sir Geoffrey Holland, a former Permanent Secretary in the Education Department, which illustrates much of the above. Every year – a good time ago – the British Safety Council used to send a telegram to the Prime Minister drawing attention to the accident rate in factories and saying that the situation warranted an enquiry. Every year the telegram was passed from Downing Street to the Secretary of State for Employment, then down through the department until it reached the desk of a middle manager who each year drafted the same defensive reply: 'The Prime Minister thanks the Safety Council for their telegram, the contents of which have been noted'. But one year the telegram was accidentally seen by a senior official called Charles Sisson who recognised the truth of the point that was being made, and penned a minute agreeing with the Council. Out of this came the Health & Safety Executive, and our whole approach to health and safety at work was modernised.

Gaining Knowledge

It cannot be emphasised strongly enough that our advice to Ministers must be based upon experience and knowledge. It should be the aim of every one of us to be the acknowledged expert in our policy area. Once we have been in the job for some time, it should be a matter of professional pride that no-one else should understand our patch better than us – and that includes Ministers and our line managers, even if they have the advantage of seeing a wider picture. Conversely, senior officials do not need to be familiar with all the detail that ought to be at the finger-tips of others. But they should be able to hold their own in any discussion of the major issues, trends and currents that affect their policy area.

> *The besetting sin of civil servants is to mix too much with each other.*
>
> Sir William Beveridge

It follows that we cannot be effective if we never get out from behind our desks. We must find a way to experience for ourselves the problems or issues with which we are dealing. Seeing, after all, is believing. We also need to be familiar with the political context of our work, and to be conscious of the world outside our own environment. Not everyone is a white collar worker, not everyone has GCSEs and not everyone lives in the South East of England. Indeed, 99 per cent of the world's population, and 96 per cent of economic activity, is outside the UK. We need to be aware of opportunities, trends and ideas outside our immediate experience. Without such experience we will never fully understand the arguments, emotions and undercurrents which condition the people and businesses with whom we deal. And only with such experience can we avoid the trap of recasting reality in our own image, and believing that our elegant and logical view represents the only possible view of the issue under consideration.

Gaining experience can also be great fun. For a start, it often involves travel. And although you might be criticised for travelling to interesting places at the taxpayer's expense, you will be criticised even more strongly – and with more reason – if you never get out at all. And you do not necessarily need to travel very far. I will certainly never forget my pre-dawn start, sorting and delivering the Royal

Mail, or the time when my secretary and I worked together on the production line at Longbridge. Both experiences taught me great respect for those who do such jobs, day in day out, without letting quality standards slip. For instance, it would have been all too easy, with a new car coming along every eighty seconds, to let a mistake go uncorrected in order to be ready for the next vehicle, but no-one did so. Such experiences also taught me the difficulty of managing in non-office environments, in out-dated buildings, and at times of day when none of us are at our best.

By the way, a good place to look for information is in the minds of front-line staff in departments and local authorities, and in the minds of others to whom the policy is directed. They will very often have a clear idea about why a situation is the way it is and why previous initiatives have failed. You should certainly never rely on middle or senior managers. For instance, Deutsche Bank asked 2.4 million customers and their branch managers and their junior branch staff, to rate branch performance. There was a very high correlation between the junior staff's perception and that of their customers, while there was almost no correlation between the branch managers' perceptions and those of their customers.

Analysing What You Have Learned

You should not, of course, simply accept all the 'facts' that are presented to you. Statistics can be particularly misleading.

- Aggregated statistics can look very different to the underlying figures. For instance, vehicle accident statistics generally include young and accident prone drivers, as well as injuries to pedestrians and cyclists. Indeed, I understand that a middle-aged car driver in good weather may well be just as safe, over most long journeys in the UK, as if he or she were flying, which is a very safe form of transport.

- The fact that there have been no incidents does not mean that something is safe. It is possible that fewer children are now killed on our roads, not because they are inherently safer than decades ago, but rather because they are so dangerous that many children are not allowed near them.
- Death and injury rates can look very different when presented as a number (e.g. number of children killed in an incident) rather than as a proportion of the exposed population per annum.
- A report of deaths caused by, for example, air pollution might include a high proportion of those whose death was already imminent, rather than deaths from amongst an otherwise healthy population.
- Isolated statistics can give a misleading impression. For instance, the radioactivity of a beach near a nuclear plant may be higher than many others, but is it also lower than other beaches which are nowhere near such a plant?

It is easy, too, to frighten people with 'science': 76 per cent of one group of adults, when presented with a number of facts about the chemical di-hydrogen monoxide, concluded that its use should be regulated by Government. The other 24 per cent presumably knew that the chemical's other name is 'water'.

Scientific 'facts' are also often anything but 'facts' as you or I would understand the term. Indeed, you can always tell good scientists by the way in which they acknowledge uncertainties, make assumptions explicit, distinguish between what is true and what is speculative, and present options.

By the way, do not be tempted, when faced with a hostile press or a one-sided lobby, to assemble your own dodgy statistics – or dodgy science – to fight them off. The inevitable result would be that you would then become seen as prejudiced and/or adversarial by those with whom you are trying to communicate, and you might also then fail to pay insufficient attention to perfectly reasonable arguments from 'the other side'.

Moving beyond science and statistics, you must remember that it is unfortunately in the nature of our society that most correspondents, and most of the people that we meet, will present a one-sided view of an issue, drawing attention to all the relevant facts and arguments which support their case but failing, either deliberately or through sheer conviction, to take account of inconvenient facts or opposing arguments. But as you gain experience, you will quickly learn to detect the pure advocate or bullshitter.

Take care, therefore, not to be too trusting and bear in mind the famous warning that 'He would say that, wouldn't he!' No one who is applying for a grant will tell you that they will in fact go ahead even if they do not get it, and no business person will tell you that the principal purpose of their latest acquisition is to build market power. Similarly, most people are reluctant to admit their errors, and their reluctance will be in proportion to the seriousness of their error. Therefore, if you are questioning the propriety of someone's behaviour, be cautious about attaching significant weight to the views of the person being questioned. Find out the facts and let them speak for themselves.

The same applies, but less strongly, to professional advisers. Lawyers, accountants and merchant bankers are employed by their clients to persuade you to do certain things. They will usually tell you the truth, but not necessarily the whole truth. They will also sometimes imply, and indeed believe, that their opinion (e.g. about the viability or prospects of a company) is a fact. If your instinct is to the contrary, then rely upon your instinct, at least to the extent of probing further.

Exploring Options

So you have identified a problem or opportunity, gained relevant experience, and identified all the necessary facts and opinions. What policy options are at your disposal?

Put shortly, the Government can do one or more of four things if it wishes to change behaviour:

- it can exhort;
- it can tax;
- it can spend – which also implies taxing or borrowing;
- it can legislate and regulate.

Exhortation means deploying all possible presentation skills, including getting key stakeholders on side, working with the media, leaflets, advertising, speeches and so on. As noted earlier, presentational issues should be considered early in any policy development process and effective presentation can sometimes achieve significant policy objectives on its own. All too often, however, you need to move on and add one of the next three options if you really want to have an impact. But then you will find that Ministers have a strong aversion to raising taxes or spending money (which are two sides of the same coin), so they prefer you to offer new legislation or regulations – until they realise that this route too can lead to huge resentment amongst those who are to be regulated, and can also have a large impact on the economy. There is much to be said, therefore, for genuinely open consultation, seeking views on the true scale of the problem and on a wide variety of ways in which it might be tackled. And don't forget to consult on the 'do nothing' option. It is often the best one! Consultation is therefore such an important process that it is worth looking at it in some detail.

Consultation

There used to be a time, apparently, when the Government could simply tell the public what decisions it had taken. It then became necessary to explain why the decision had been taken, which in turn led Ministers to consult in advance of decision-making. Best practice is now to go even further and involve the public and key stakeholders at all stages of the policy process.

There are lots of different ways to do this and you should not simply duplicate what someone else has done before you. In particular, don't limit yourself to written communications. Discussion groups, large formal meetings, informal meetings with individuals and the Internet all have a part to play. And even when preparing formal written consultation, there are a number of choices. Have a look at the detailed advice that is available on consultation procedures, and also look at a range of previous consultation documents and choose a format which best suits your needs. Above all, remember that you are in policy-formulation or policy-implementation mode, so there is no need to be defensive. Indeed, you should positively encourage respondents to point out your mistakes and possible pitfalls. If your process is effective, and you take the responses seriously, you will find that you then avoid a very large number of traps that you would not have spotted by yourself.

You should also strongly encourage those who seem to be able to take a wider view. Cultivate those who say unexpected things or comment candidly upon their organisation. Such people shine unaccustomed light on issues and can be invaluable contributors to the policy making process. Above all, talk to those who are unhappy with your policies. They often have a good reason, which you need to bear in mind whether or not you can change the policy, or its detail, as a result. And don't hesitate to let your Minister have short note of what you have learned. It might just make him or her think twice.

If the subject of your consultation is particularly controversial, or if you are to meet a potentially hostile audience, or hostile media, you should remember the following basic rules:

- Actions speak louder than words. The vast majority of your audience will respond wholly or mainly to the way in which you deliver your message. 'Organisational body language' is important. Do you act, write or sound patronising, worried and harassed? Or do you act and sound calm, sympathetic and in control?

- Do not dismiss concerns, however silly you think they sound. If it appears that you do not respect basic human concerns, how can you then be trusted to come up with sensible policies?

- Instead, listen carefully and emphasise your own concern. Then commit to continuing speedy enquiries, taking proper advice and reaching an early sensible conclusion on the best way forward. Stress that the process will be participative and open, and that you will publish any scientific or other expert advice and the assumptions upon which it is based. Remember that the public will trust you much more if you admit to uncertainty, and that the public may well be less concerned about the problem than the media.

- Explain the benefits of your proposed approach. Stress that your reaction to any problem will not be 'knee-jerk', and you will not patronise or nanny the public. If regulation might be needed, explain how this will protect the public and why other options would not work. If regulation is likely to be unnecessary, stress that you believe it right that the public should be allowed to make their own assessment of the problem, and the associated costs, risks and benefits, and react as they wish.

- A small but crucial minority in your audience will be opinion formers who will want to understand the underlying issues and will analyse your response very carefully. Get the majority of them to accept your credibility, and respect your openness, and they will sustain you against much unfair comment.

- Do not say that a particular option would be 'too expensive'. Who are you to say that?

- Do not express concern that action to protect the public would harm industry, for this will reinforce any concern that a risk is being transferred from those who are benefiting from it onto those who are not.

- Membership of advisory groups should be broadly based, and not confined to scientists and other professionals.

- When dealing with risks to health and safety, remember that nothing in this world is entirely 'safe'. The Government's job is to ensure that everything is 'safe enough'.

Finally, remember that there is a crucial difference between releasing information and informing the public. The wholesale release of vast amounts of data does not of itself inform anyone. There should of course be no question of hiding or distorting information, but care should be taken to ensure that the overall effect of the release of information is to improve recipients' understanding of the issues (and the uncertainties) rather than simply to add to the confusion.

Regulatory Impact Assessment
Good process is usually an indispensable part of achieving a good outcome, and this is never more so than in the case of the Regulatory Impact Assessment (RIA) which must be carried out as

an integral part of the evidence based policy making process. The Cabinet Office provides excellent clear advice in this area, which you should certainly read as soon as you start thinking about tackling a policy issue. The key points, some of which have also been made earlier in this chapter, are as follows.

- First, consider – and that means seriously consider – all the options, from doing nothing through to legislation, with improving information, codes of practice, self-regulation and economic incentives along the way.
- Second, consult – and that means consult before making firm recommendations to Ministers as well as, for instance, on any draft legislation.
- Third, if you do need to legislate, keep the regulations as simple as you can. Identify the precise problem, use plain English, provide flexibility and keep it short!
- Fourth, consider compliance (see further below).
- Fifth, provide good, clear, simple guidance to accompany the regulations.
- Sixth, if regulation appears necessary, prepare a formal Regulatory Impact Assessment at each stage. The first – for Whitehall use only – should include a clear statement of the policy objectives as well as an initial assessment of the risks, costs and benefits of regulation, as well as why non-regulatory options – including doing nothing – are unattractive. Later assessments will build on these foundations, adding more detail and more certainty, and they will be published as part of the formal consultation process and alongside draft legislation. It cannot be stressed too strongly that RIAs are very important documents, whose preparation needs to be properly planned and resourced, and started early enough to form a genuine part of the decision making process.

Much the same advice applies if you are negotiating in Brussels. Again, the Cabinet Office offers excellent guidance, and either you or the Commission should prepare a *fiche d'impact* – the Euro version of a Regulatory Impact Assessment.

Transposition/Gold plating

You will also have choices when it comes to transposing European Directives into UK law. The process can be fraught with difficulty, and legal advice should be obtained as soon as you begin to think about transposition, which should in turn be very early in the negotiation process.

You need to reconcile a number of possible tensions. One source of tension is the desire of those who are to be regulated for regulatory certainty. Small firms in particular do not want to have to go to court to resolve ambiguities or to find out how the law applies to unusual circumstances. So even if the Directive itself is not very detailed (and they often are) you end up drafting to cope with every eventuality, whereupon everyone complains about the length and complexity of your proposal. It is truly a no-win situation.

Another tension arises when you try to define the businesses, employees and activities that are within the scope of the UK regulation. EU legislators often kindly leave such decisions, within limits, to national governments, but this can be a poisoned chalice. If you spread your net too wide then you will again be accused of over-regulating and 'gold-plating' the Directive. But if you exempt things which you could have caught, you are then likely to face a legal challenge from the Commission or from someone who might have benefited from a wider interpretation.

There is therefore often no risk-free route to implementation and you must offer Ministers a range of strategies and help them choose the right one in all the circumstances. You should in particular not necessarily recommend the option which is legally watertight. It can often be wise to take a small risk of legal challenge in return for coming up with a solution which makes sense within our economy and society, even if it is not the route chosen by other member states.

Unwanted Consequences

It is also important, whether you are imposing taxes, spending money, drafting domestic legislation or transposing European legislation, that you take care to avoid unwanted consequences, and (if regulations are necessary) to regulate in such a way as to encourage compliance and deter evasion. Let's look first at unwanted consequences.

The key point to remember is that it can be very difficult to identify such consequences – and this is one of the main reasons why genuinely open-minded consultation is so important. It might help if I list the sort of unwanted consequence that can occur:

- A risk-free food chain might raise costs (to the detriment of the poor), restrict imports (to the detriment of the third world) or sacrifice taste and texture for the monotonous security of the can.
- Attempts to reduce sports injuries might well generate poor health as a result of reduced physical activity.
- Expensive railway safety might increase fares and charges and so divert traffic to more dangerous urban roads.
- Attempts to create risk-free child-care might reduce the availability of such care.
- The risk to a child living with inadequate parents needs to be balanced against the risk of the damage that would arise from enforced separation.
- UK-only regulation might, if it were to increase the price of UK goods, lead to cheap unregulated goods coming in from abroad.

It is also important to remember that you are dealing with a dynamic situation, not a static laboratory experiment. For instance, because we each seek to arrive at our personal balance between cost and benefit, we will intuitively adjust our behaviour to avoid, or mitigate the effect of an increased risk, and vice versa for a reduced risk. The observed effect of an increased or reduced risk is therefore often unpredictable. This particularly applies where (as in the case of road safety) most of us have intuitively established the level of risk with which we feel comfortable. To take a simple example, if a winding road is to be straightened or widened, you would not assume that drivers (or the NHS) would pocket the value of all the increased safety. Instead, most drivers would speed up – accepting some of the risk for themselves, and transferring some of the risk to pedestrians etc.

Another aspect of the same phenomenon is that the public or business community will usually adjust their behaviour to cope with an unwelcome development, or simply just get used to it. This is why environmental groups, for instance, are so keen to stop certain developments before they become established as precedents. Their response may seem to be out of proportion to the harm done by the proposed development but it might make a great deal of sense in the wider scheme of things. Do not therefore underestimate or patronise such lobby groups.

Indeed, once a policy decision has been implemented, it can be very difficult to tell whether it was correct, and it also becomes very difficult to get back to where you began. Who knows, for instance, whether it was right to give planning permission to certain large developments? But any attempt to knock them down would cause an uproar, from those who live in, work in or supply them, or from those who have simply grown fond of them (Battersea Power Station, for instance). I sometimes wonder what would have happened if our predecessors had known for certain that motor vehicles would end up causing one million deaths a year around the world. So don't get too upset when a Minister takes an apparently illogical decision. The Great British Public will probably find a way of adjusting to the decision, if not actually circumventing it.

Compliance

It is also vital that compliance and enforcement issues are considered before any decisions are made about the scope and nature of any regulations. The legislation can be well-meant, but it will quickly fall into disrepute if it has to be policed in an obtrusive way, or if the cost of its enforcement is out of proportion to its benefit. Regulations should always be transparent, targeted, consistent, and in proportion to the risk, and the regulator must be publicly accountable.

Compliance is often best assured by providing incentives to encourage those causing the risk to change their behaviour. Where possible, therefore, the cost or impact of the regulation should fall upon the person causing the risk, not the person suffering it. If that is not possible then any numerical targets (e.g. for local enforcement bodies) should be concerned with reductions in the occurrence in the risk (e.g. fewer outbreaks of food poisoning) rather than increases in enforcement action (e.g. numbers of prosecutions). And don't make it obligatory for small firms to keep papers for 40 years – and, yes, such a regulation did recently exist.

Watch out, by the way, for the implications for middle class journalists. For instance, when designing policies affecting employees, think carefully about their impact on au pairs. Or when changing education policy, how will it affect Montessori schools? You attack the freedom of the press at your peril!

Finally, make sure that your solution can be implemented by those who have not been immersed in the issue in the way that you have been. Don't design systems which are subtle, clever or difficult to understand, and don't plan staff numbers and implementation timetables on the basis that all involved will be geniuses. Also, make sure that your solution is understood by those at whom it is aimed. Research can help, of course. The DTI, investigating ineffective product warnings, found that many young people could not define the word 'fatal'. A new warning 'solvent abuse can kill suddenly' was substituted.

Navigating Whitehall

We are now near the end of the policy process, but you still have to steer your excellent and innovative solution through the Whitehall machine. Scylla and Charybdis have nothing on the traps that can befall you in this part of the process. I return to the subject of innovation later on, but it is worth mentioning here that the main obstacles to an innovative solution will be as follows:

- Because the Government works in an adversarial environment, new ideas are swiftly attacked, improvements are regarded as evidence of past failure, and debates about the merits of particular proposals are seized upon as signs of division within Government.
- We work within quite distinct Government departments, with quite distinct budgets, and for Ministers who are usually in competition with their colleagues in other departments. This encourages an over-exaggerated loyalty to the organisation, to our staff, to our budget and to our Ministers, and elementary game theory teaches us that, if no-one else is co-operating, it is not in our interests to co-operate with them.
- It is a firm rule that the Treasury have to be consulted before we commit resource to anything 'novel or contentious'. And if that

doesn't stop us in our tracks, a colleague will soon remind us that our Permanent Secretary is directly accountable to Parliament for the way in which we spend public money. You will not be encouraged to innovate in a way which could cause him or her to have to defend you in front of the Public Accounts Committee.

- Common sense, bolstered by the doctrine of collective responsibility, means that it is necessary to consult, often quite widely, before becoming committed to any significant new policy. Colleagues will inevitably express various concerns and, although it might be possible to address each of them, the effort of doing so can be quite daunting.

There is no easy or simple route between these obstacles, but some lessons seem to have general applicability.

First, you need to put real effort into building a strong partnership with your Minister, backed by the Secretary of State. Private Secretaries and Special Advisers can be very helpful here.

Next, involve colleagues from other departments, including the Treasury, at the earliest possible opportunity, and try to build loyalty to the project, as distinct from natural loyalty to departmental Ministers. Remember that 'joining up' becomes more difficult the more you involve Ministers and senior officials, so tackle this problem early, not late. Encourage your opposite numbers in other departments to get their bosses and their Minister on board, and get your Minister to talk to theirs, assuming the two of them get on reasonably well. Seek at all times to ensure that the initiative is seen as cross-departmental.

Tackle the resources issue up front. Many Ministers do not like to get involved in resource allocation, believing that civil servants should sort this out. But the absence of resources – whether staff or money – can be a big problem. Don't whine to your Minister, of course, but put up a lean project plan with necessary resources clearly identified, and get it backed. You will have to get your finance people to comment on your plans – and if they say that they cannot be afforded then your Minister will have to decide whether to fight for new money. But let that be the Minister's decision, not yours, and not your finance branch's. Don't let Ministers complain that you never deliver, if the truth is that they will not find the money.

Plan your consultation and media strategy with particular care. It is usually a very bad idea to be secretive. It is much better to start discussing the idea, in a non-committal low-key way, with key interest groups, with academia and with the specialist press. This allows you to confront the problems very early on, and gets buy-in from key stakeholders. And such openness then makes it more difficult for the national press later to run shock-horror stories.

Keep colleagues – and especially senior colleagues – well informed. None of them like surprises, so tell them about the initiative, and assure them that there is strong Ministerial support. Also tell them whenever another key group or opinion-former comes on board. They will be glad to be associated with success, and less likely to cause problems.

Build a strong, diverse team, and try to involve outside stakeholders as much as possible. Build partnerships not only within government but also with local authorities, the private and voluntary sectors, with other EU member states and so on. And make sure that a good proportion of your team have strong interpersonal skills, for these are necessary if these partnerships are to be truly effective.

Keep the thing moving. It can be difficult to regain lost momentum, and there are real lost opportunities, and real costs, associated with delay, even if they do not fall on your budget.

Will you need Ministers to take a Bill through Parliament? If so, plan ahead. There is quite a queue!

Above all, have a clear, written strategy and project plan, kept up to date (for it will often change) and available to all those involved. If you can publish it on the Internet, so much the better.

The Final Stages

The key things to think about are collective agreement (of which more below), legislation, guidance material and presentation, including media handling.

If you need primary legislation – that is a Bill which becomes an Act of Parliament - then you need to build this into your timetable right from the start. You need drafting authority before Parliamentary Counsel can be set to work, and you then need specific collective agreement before your Bill finds its way into the programme. It is all complex but well-trodden ground, beyond the scope of these notes. But there are plenty of people who are willing to help, and plenty of high quality guidance material, which you ignore at your peril.

Explaining your new policy or initiative to the public, should be straightforward if you have successfully involved stakeholder groups who will have stopped you making everything too complex. But do prepare draft guidance material well in advance of final announcement, for you will find that the process of seeking to explain your decisions will quickly identify where you have made mistakes.

Presenting your new policy, including media handling, should also be fairly straightforward, if you have followed the advice in this book and considered presentational issues right from the beginning of the policy development process. It also helps if you have managed to avoid the worst of the obstacles to innovation summarised earlier in this chapter. But don't forget that your Minister will certainly want a launch of some sort, which you and your Press Office should jointly organise.

Gaining Collective Agreement

Ministers take a great many different types of decision, and the majority of these are of interest to Ministers in only one or two departments, often including the Treasury. However, Ministers need to gain the collective agreement of every department if their proposals:

- are likely to attract significant Parliamentary, media or other attention, e.g. from lobby groups, and/or
- are unwelcome to Ministers in another department, and/or
- require primary legislation, and/or
- need to be trailed in a Green or White Paper.

If you are embarking on this process for the first time then you should look at the voluminous written guidance, and there is also much to be said for mimicking the style and structure of letters and papers prepared previously. Collective agreement is obtained through Cabinet committees, usually through correspondence or, in particularly difficult cases, in meetings. The impartial Committee Secretariats will tell you how best to proceed but, in the case of correspondence, the process usually involves your Minister writing to the Chair of the appropriate committee and copying the letter to all other committee members. Your Minister's Private Secretary should extract replies, or nil returns, from all committee members and you should then contact the Secretariat to confirm that the correspondence is complete. If all goes well, the Secretariat will get the Chair to write to confirm the collective decision to go ahead, perhaps on certain terms. Otherwise, you or your Minister will have to resolve points of disagreement, before writing round again with a collectively acceptable proposal.

It is vital that both correspondence and papers should (in the case of significant, novel or contentious expenditure proposals) contain the views of the Treasury and (in the case of proposals impacting significantly on the private or voluntary sectors) contain a statement agreed with the Regulatory Impact Unit in the Cabinet Office.

If a dispute cannot be settled through inter-departmental correspondence and discussions, the Secretariat will arrange for the committee to meet and consider a paper which you will prepare, consulting those colleagues in other departments who have strong views on the issue. The paper should not be too long – three to five sides (plus annexes) is quite long enough – and it should outline the proposal, the main considerations that Ministers need to bear in mind, and a precise statement of the decisions sought. Any inter-departmental disagreements should be summarised in a neutral way.

A Policy Checklist

Annex 2 to this book contains a useful checklist which encapsulates much of the above advice – and more besides. Copies can also be downloaded from www.civilservant.org.uk.

4   The European Union

It is hard, these days, to find a policy area that could never become the subject of a discussion at the European level. The following chapter gives advice on working effectively in Europe, and summarises some key facts about the structure of the institutions.

Major differences

The EU is neither a traditional international organisation like the UN or the OECD, nor is it a true nation state like France or the United Kingdom. Rather, it is a new and different form of association, which needs to be understood on its own terms and not by comparison to other, perhaps more familiar models. This is particularly important when looking at European legislation, which is binding and is often agreed by some form of majority voting. This, along with the fact that European law has supremacy over national law – in other words, if the two conflict, then European law wins out – makes for a very different dynamic.

Working the European Union machine is therefore quite different to working the Whitehall machine. Some of the more obvious differences between the UK and 'Europe' are as follows:

- Within the UK Parliamentary system, Parliament and the Government are uniquely powerful. Within Europe, both Ministers and officials are negotiators, applicants or supplicants.

- There is no UK equivalent of the Qualified Majority Voting (QMV) system, or of the need for unanimity.
- The practical application of our negotiating strength can be troublesome. For instance, if there is a need for unanimity then in theory we have a veto. But it is not expected that anyone should use the veto at all frequently. Rather it is a card that can from time to time be played to achieve a national objective. If we do not recognise this, then others will not make concessions to the UK, since nothing can be secured in return, and bad feelings will spill over into other areas.
- Where QMV applies, our strength is even more circumscribed. One country alone cannot block progress and usually will be isolated if it tries. This can lead to a less palatable result than constructive engagement would have achieved.
- There is no UK equivalent of the Council of Ministers or the Commission. It is a great mistake to treat the Commission as though it were simply some sort of supra-national civil service – it clearly also has a political role.
- Commission officials tend to be very good or rather poor, with rather fewer moderate performers than one might expect.
- The Commission is very vertically organised, so that there is often poor working level co-ordination within the Commission, whether between or within directorates-general. This gives great power to the cabinets of the various Commissioners.
- It is also notable that the Commissioners, their cabinets and their officials ('Services') are very open – arguably more accessible to lobbyists and industry than their equivalents in national governments. Partly because the Services are thinly staffed, they have very little information of their own. It can be very helpful if you are the person who briefs them. But watch out for competitive lobbying from the opposition, whoever they may be.
- Relations between civil servants and Members of the European

Parliament are also different. Unlike within Westminster, direct contact with MEPs of all parties (and all countries) is not only allowed, it is to be encouraged.

- UKRep too (our permanent representatives in Brussels and Luxembourg) are very happy to meet and help British lobbyists who need advice on operating the Brussels machine.
- EU officials in the Council, Commission and Parliament are almost always very pro-European, as are a large number of your opposite numbers in other national delegations. Even if you hate the very idea of European integration or the single currency, you may find you get a more receptive audience to your lobbying if you hide your views and couch your comments and arguments in 'communautaire' (EU-friendly) language.

Lobbying and Informal Contacts

For a civil servant working in a policy area with a European dimension, lobbying and information gathering has no beginning and no end – it should be a continuous, planned process whose focus shifts according to the state of play of a particular dossier.

- Get in early. EU policies are like supertankers – a small nudge early on can make a huge difference to the end position, but the later you leave it the harder you have to push to make any difference at all. Produce the first bit of paper, and you have set the agenda.
- Maintain good personal contacts with Commission and other Member State officials, relevant industry groups and other interested parties (consumer groups, NGOs, etc). Not only does this mean you'll have a better understanding of their position, but it will also increase the chances of you hearing about new developments in the policy area early on. If your contacts respect you,

you will also be better placed to put your point of view across.

- You should identify and build alliances with opposite numbers in other Member States. (You should use UKRep and other Embassies to help develop those alliances.) But don't just talk to 'friends' – after all, it is not them you need to convince!

- Don't forget the European Parliament! This institution has a very important influence over the European agenda, with the vast majority of legislation jointly adopted by it and the Council. Identify the key MEPs in your policy area (UKRep can help a lot here) – often those on the relevant committee – and develop a relationship with them. Often, you can be one of their most reliable sources of information and facts.

- Effective lobbying is a two-way street. Always try to be able to offer some information on others' positions or facts about the issue at hand in exchange for what you want.

- Get UK industry to make full use of Europe-wide trade associations in lobbying the Commission, and encourage them to get their opposite numbers in other countries to seek support from their national governments.

- Consult interested parties in the UK. In addition to keeping them up to date with progress, the information they can give you on likely effects will inform both your lobbying and negotiating strategies and offer alternative ways of achieving the same end. Consider all forms of consultation, not just a formal documents – focus groups; email lists; web sites; workshops; seminars; etc.

- It is often helpful to get other Government departments on your side. The Treasury can be particularly helpful e.g. in lobbying other Finance Ministries against state aids.

- Do not forget to lobby cabinets as well as the Services: the two operate fairly independently. UKRep will help you do this.

Formal Negotiation

Formal negotiation takes place first of all at a technical level in Council working groups. Here, officials from all the Member States and the Commission, chaired by the Presidency, seek to resolve as many of the issues as possible. When they have achieved all they can, the dossier will be passed up to COREPER (the Committee of Permanent Representatives) and then to Ministers in the Council for final agreement (or referral back for more work!).

Even before taking part in a working group:

- You should have a clear, prioritised strategy, agreed by Ministers. Ideally this will have already informed your lobbying activities.
- Try to avoid taking up an inflexible negotiating position. Outright opposition to a measure will mean that UK concerns about the shape and detail of a draft directive will be ignored to the detriment of the UK. It is often much better to engage with other Member States on the detail of the proposal in order to achieve as good a result as possible.
- You may not personally believe in European integration. But any argument based on anything approaching Euroscepticism risks almost immediate dismissal. However, this doesn't mean that the national interest doesn't matter. There is generally a great deal of willingness to accommodate particular national difficulties. Wherever possible, back up your arguments with facts – often obtained through national consultation.
- Be aware of the dynamic of the negotiation. The very beginning is usually the time for declarations of principle, but things move quickly into discussions of detail. As the process accelerates and the pressure to reach agreement grows it becomes almost impossible to introduce new elements or to try to reopen points already agreed.
- Know when to give up on a point that is of little real importance.

Multiple interventions on minor points of detail can quickly exhaust the patience of others around the table, and can often best be dealt with by a quiet word with the Presidency or the General Secretariat.

- Try to keep a feel for that intangible but vital commodity, negotiating capital. Making concessions on items you have portrayed as important to you earns you capital. Winning a point (or even fighting it too hard) spends it.

- Aim to maintain your informal contacts and use them between formal sessions and, where appropriate, in the margins of those sessions too. Generally, the best way to garner support is to float an idea informally first, then, when you have secured sufficient support (usually involving the Presidency and, if at all possible, the Commission), raise it in a formal session.

- Don't forget that what you are negotiating is law. Keep close contact with your lawyers to make sure the text really does mean what you think it does. They can also help you keep in mind how the text before you will be turned into national law. Negotiation and transposition are not separate processes, and the need for fair but effective enforcement must be addressed whilst directives are being negotiated.

Structure

You can survive quite well in Brussels without understanding every last detail of the treaties and structures. But it is best to have the following basic knowledge if you want to be truly effective.

In existence since the Maastricht Treaty of 1992, the European Union (the EU) consists of three 'pillars', supported by common institutions. The three pillars are:

- The two European Communities, which are:
    a) The European Atomic Energy Community.
    b) The European Community (the EC), previously the European Economic Community.
- Common Foreign and Security Policy
- Police and Judicial Co-operation

The second and third pillars have a somewhat less direct impact on UK legislation and, unless you work in the Home Office, the Ministry of Defence or the Foreign Office, they are unlikely to concern you. Also, the European Atomic Energy Community is of specialist interest only, so the most important element within the EU is the EC. Note that the EC still exists and it is not the same as the EU, and that we are subject to much EC (but not to EU) legislation. However, most people refer to EU legislation and it is not generally worth correcting them.

There are two other key structures:

- 13 Member States (i.e. all except the UK, Ireland and the 2004 accession countries) plus Iceland and Norway have removed all internal border controls (and are generally referred to as the Schengen area after the Convention that originally introduced this approach).
- 12 Member States (not the UK, Denmark or Sweden) had by early 2004 entered into Economic and Monetary Union (EMU) and adopted the Single Currency (the Euro), on terms agreed in the Treaty of Maastricht in 1992. Those states joining the Union after this date are expected to adopt the Euro as soon as they can.

Current membership of the Schengen Area and EMU can be found at www.civilservant.org.uk.

Institutions

For most purposes, there are five main institutions that influence the Union in various ways.

1. *The Council of the European Union* is, with the Parliament, the main law-making and decision-making body in the EU. It is often referred to as 'The Council Of Ministers' and should not be confused with the Council of Europe, which was established after the Second World War with the aim of protecting Europe against totalitarianism.

The Council brings together representatives of all the Member State governments and is the forum in which these representatives assert their interests and reach compromises. These meetings happen regularly at a range of levels – expert officials from capitals, diplomats from the Permanent Representations (broadly speaking, Embassies), Ministers and, usually about four times a year, at the level of Presidents and Prime Ministers in the European Council (summit).

Ministerial Council meetings (Environment, Competitiveness, Agriculture, etc.) take place between 1 and 15 times a year, depending on the Council. Each meeting is attended by the appropriate Minister from each Member State (or their permanent representative) and the relevant Commissioner. The Council is chaired by a rotating Presidency from amongst the Member States (of which more below) – changing every six months. Most of the work is done in the 300 plus working groups, which in turn feed into COREPER – the Committee of Permanent Representatives – and thence to Ministers. The Council is also assisted by a permanent staff called the General Secretariat of the Council, not to be confused with the Secretariat-General of the Commission.

The Council (usually together with the European Parliament) agrees legislation, budgets and other rules for most of the more familiar activities of the EU, such as the single market, common policies like those on agriculture and fishing, environmental protection, trade and the free movement of goods, persons, services and money.

In addition, the Council is the main EU institution responsible for intergovernmental cooperation on common foreign and security policy (assisted by the High Representative for common foreign and security policy) and on justice and home affairs.

The Presidency of the Council can have quite an influential role. It sets the agenda for the six months it is at the helm – which includes the possibility to not address matters it does not like. Current and forthcoming Presidencies are listed at .

Many important external issues are dealt with by the 'Troika' – the previous, current and next Presidencies. In addition, there is a High Representative for foreign and security (second pillar) matters.

Most Council decisions are taken by Qualified Majority Voting (QMV). The current definition of a 'qualified majority' and the number of votes currently available to be cast by each member state may be found at www.civilservant.co.uk.

2. *The European Parliament* (EP), which usually shares decision-making with the Council, is made up of directly elected representatives from the Member States (732 from the June 2004 elections), roughly in proportion to population. Most decisions are prepared in committees (usually in Brussels) and finally voted on in the regular plenary sessions (usually in Strasbourg).

The Parliament's principal roles are to:

• examine and adopt European legislation. Most legislation is now agreed under the codecision procedure, where Parliament shares power with the Council;

- approve the EU budget;
- exercise democratic control over the other EU institutions, for example by setting up committees of inquiry;
- assent to important international agreements such as the accession of new EU Member States and trade or association agreements between the EU and other countries.

As with national parliaments, the EP has specialist committees to deal with particular issues (foreign affairs, budget, environment and so on). Most of its work is in fact done through these committees.

3. *The European Commission* is (from October 2004) headed by 25 senior figures, one from each of the member states, but formally independent of national allegiance, making up the college of Commissioners. Each has a small group of officials – the cabinet – to assist them monitor and drive the development of policy. The President of the Commission or one of his two Vice-Presidents chairs their weekly meetings. A staff of about 24,000 divided between 36 Directorates-General and Services (including the Secretariat-General, Press and translation service) supports the college.

The European Commission does much of the day-to-day work in the European Union. In most areas of EU business it is the only body that can draft proposals for new legislation, which it presents to the European Parliament and the Council. The Commission makes sure that EU decisions are properly implemented and supervises the way EU funds are spent. It is also charged with ensuring that everyone abides by the European treaties and European law. With the major exception of competition policy, it doesn't generally have a large role in actual implementation or enforcement – this is primarily a Member State responsibility. In certain areas (see the section on competence later), the Commission also has the role of representing the EU in external (i.e. with non-EU countries) negotiations and meetings.

4. The European Court of Justice (in Luxembourg, not to be confused with the non-EU bodies, the European Court of Human Rights, in Strasbourg and the International Court of Justice in The Hague) is the final arbiter of all questions of European law. The ECJ, as everyone calls it, ensures the consistent and accurate interpretation of European law across the EU. If national courts are in doubt about how to apply EU rules they must ask the Court of Justice. Member States, certain EU institutions and individuals can also bring proceedings against EU institutions before the Court. Some less significant cases can also be heard by its subsidiary court, the Court of First Instance. The ECJ consists of one independent judge from each EU country.

5. The European Court of Auditors, also located in Luxembourg, is the body that checks how EU money is spent, both directly by other institutions and, where appropriate, by Member States (for example agricultural subsidies or regional development aid).

These five key institutions are flanked by five other bodies of varying importance:

- The European Central Bank (responsible for monetary policy and managing the euro);
- The Economic and Social Committee (expresses the opinions of organised civil society on economic and social issues);
- The Committee of the Regions (expresses the opinions of regional and local authorities);
- The Ombudsman (deals with citizens' complaints about malad-

ministration by any EU institution or body);

- The European Investment Bank (helps achieve EU objectives by financing investment projects).

A large number of agencies (such as the European Medicines Evaluation Agency, European Food Safety Authority and so on) and other bodies complete the system.

Key Dates

1952	Treaty of Paris (1951) between Belgium, France, Germany, Italy, Luxembourg and the Netherlands enters into force. European Coal and Steel Community (ECSC) created.
1958	Treaties of Rome (1957) enter into force. Euratom and EEC (later renamed the EC) created.
1973	Denmark, Ireland and UK join the communities.
1981	Greece joins.
1986	Portugal and Spain join.
1987	Single European Act (1986) enters into force.
1993	Maastricht Treaty (1992) enters into force. EU created.
1993	Single Market 'completed'.
1995	Austria, Finland and Sweden join the EU, bringing the total to 15.
1999	Amsterdam Treaty (1997) enters into force.
1999	Economic and Monetary Union starts.
2000	Pre-enlargement Inter-governmental Conference (IGC) starts.
2002	Treaty of Paris (and hence the ECSC) expires.
2002	Introduction of Euro coins and notes.
2004	Enlargement: Cyprus, Czech Republic, Estonia, Hungary,

Latvia, Lithuania, Malta, Poland, Slovakia, Slovenia all join, bringing the total to 25.

Legislation

There are five kinds of 'act' that can be adopted. Opinions and Recommendations are non-binding guidance. Decisions are binding in their entirety upon those to whom they are addressed (individuals, companies, countries). Regulations are binding in their entirety and are generally and directly applicable in all Member States. Directives set out the result to be achieved but leave the choice of form and methods to the national authorities in each Member State to which they are addressed – in other words, they always require transposition into national law.

Codecision

Most EC legislation is adopted through a process called codecision. This can be quite a complex procedure, but the basic outline is given below. Be careful though – this is a simplified description and there can be many twists and turns on the road, and some steps may happen more or less at the same time. In addition, if all parties agree, the process can be stopped at any point after the European Parliament's (EP) First Reading and the proposal adopted.

- The Commission makes a proposal for legislation to the EP and the Council.
- The EP gives its First Reading opinion on the proposal, in the form of a series of amendments. (Note that the opinion is adopted on the basis of a simple majority of MEPs voting in the plenary session.)
- The Commission gives its views on the EP's amendments and

changes its proposal accordingly.

- The Council adopts its Common Position, taking into consideration the EP's amendments. The voting is usually by Qualified Majority (though sometimes unanimity applies throughout) if the Commission concurs, otherwise unanimity is needed. It then forwards the Common Position to the EP, along with an explanation of its reasons.

- The EP then has three months to examine the Common Position, along with the Commission's views on it. Within this period it adopts its Second Reading amendments. This time only amendments achieving the support of an absolute majority of MEPs (that is, half of all MEPs plus one) go through.

- The Council now has three months to decide which of the EP amendments it will take on board. The Council can usually adopt those amendments on which the Commission has expressed a positive opinion by QMV (though sometimes unanimity applies throughout), but the Council needs unanimity for those where the Commission has expressed a negative opinion. If all amendments are accepted, the process ends and the proposal is adopted.

- If one or more amendments are rejected, then conciliation starts. The Conciliation Committee must meet within six weeks of the rejection and reach a conclusion within a further six weeks. It is made up of representatives of the Member States (usually chaired by a Minister, with other Member States represented by the Permanent Representative or his deputy) plus an equal number of MEPs. The Commission is tasked with assisting the Committee.

- If conciliation is successful, the Council (QMV or sometimes unanimity) and the EP (absolute majority) must each then adopt the modified text within another six weeks.

Comitology

Once legislation has been agreed, there will often be an ongoing need to update it to account for technical progress/changes, to oversee its implementation and to draw up guidance. This is generally done by the Commission, assisted (or interfered with, depending on your point of view) by a committee made up of representatives of the Member States. This goes by the delightfully uninformative name of comitology and can have significant effects on policy in the UK.

Potential Implications for National Policy

'Competence'

The first key question you need to ask is whether or not there is EU competence in this policy area. This is the jargon phrase for whether or not the EU already has a role/responsibility in a particular area, and if so how much of one. Some areas are of exclusive competence for the EU – the EU is the only body with the right to develop policy in this area and the Commission speaks for the EU. The best examples here are agriculture and international trade. One good (but alas not definitive) clue is if people talk about a 'Common XXX Policy'. Other areas of policy are of mixed competence for the EU – it has a significant role, but so do the Member States and they can speak for themselves in international discussions. Good examples include environmental policy and development aid. The third category, logically, is that of national competence, where the EU has no significant role (often being limited to information exchange, exhortation, and so on). Examples here are military matters, healthcare provision and education. It is also true to say that there is a tendency over time for the EU to try to extend its competence – to transform mixed competence into exclusive and national competence into mixed.

In attempting to answer the competence question, you must remember that even in the areas of pure national competence there can be overspill. Just because you are commissioning a brand new hospital (healthcare provision), it doesn't mean you can ignore EU rules on public procurement or state aids! If there is exclusive EU competence, then the probable implication is that you cannot do anything at a national level that has a legal effect, and even some exhortation or tax/spend options may not be feasible. Your main option in this instance is to try to persuade the EU to act as you would like, which has its own problems and risks.

If there is mixed competence then you will probably need more expert advice as to whether there is a conflict or not, usually from your lawyers. If there is no conflict, or only national competence, and there is no overspill, then off you go! However, you may wish to consider checking with the Commission to ensure it also agrees there is no problem (it'll probably find out about the policy sooner or later – many Commission officials regularly listen to the *Today* programme and read the *Financial Times* – so best to make sure there won't be problems down the line). You may also want to keep the Commission and/or other Member States informed of what you are doing, especially if you might be able to learn something from their experience or if you might at some stage want to export your ideas to the European level.

Other typical EU issues that may arise with implications for national policy are:

- *Transposition/Gold plating* This issue considered in the Policy Process chapter of this book.
- *State aids* (subsidies) – giving support in cash or kind to someone in a way or for purposes that run counter to the rules on state aids;

- *Public procurement* (purchasing goods and services by the state, broadly defined) – there are some strict rules requiring companies from other Member States to find out about and tender for significant public procurement on an equal basis;
- *Free movement of goods, services, labour and capital* – there is a general prohibition on establishing legal or practical barriers to these 'four freedoms' without good reason, such as public security, or protection of the environment. In some areas, failure to notify such barriers to the Commission can result in them being invalid and unenforceable in the courts. (This follows a case in the Netherlands where failure to notify technical standards for supply of breathalysers resulted in all who had been convicted of drink driving on the basis of tests by those breathalysers having their convictions quashed…!)
- *Environmental impact* – there are rules on carrying out environmental impact assessments on a range of projects;
- *Competition law* – deliberately or accidentally putting up barriers to competition.

5   Parliamentary Business

The defining characteristics of any profession are that its members are accountable to others, and that their behaviour is constrained by ethical rules which ensure that its members act primarily in the interest of others rather than themselves. The civil service is, therefore, certainly a profession, for we are accountable in many different ways and bound by a wide variety of codes and rules. And although the constraints seem daunting, you should bear in mind that there is nothing in them that stops us achieving things, as long as we respect the rules, and understand the reasons for them. Indeed, the best civil servants are surely those who show that they can get things done without bending or ignoring the constraints within which we must work.

Details of the principal constraints are in the following two chapters. The first of these deals with Ministers' and officials' principal accountability, which is to Parliament. This takes two forms. First, Parliament can question and debate both policies and behaviour. Second, it exercises close control over Government expenditure.

It might be helpful to start by understanding the Parliamentary timetable, which is summarised below.

A new Parliament begins after a general election. A new Parliamentary Session begins with the Queen's Speech in November each year, and, in the absence of an election, runs through to the following October, with a big gap for the Summer recess. Bills cannot normally be carried over from one session to another but there are a growing number of exceptions to this rule, about which you can get advice from your Parliamentary Branch. A new Parliamentary term begins after the Christmas, Easter and Summer recesses.

The Parliamentary day typically begins at either 10.30am or 2.30pm with prayers. Officials are not allowed into 'the box' near their Ministers until five minutes later when First in Order Oral Questions begin (usually abbreviated to First Order PQs or Oral PQs). These finish at 11.30 or 3.30, or 12.00 noon on a Wednesday when they are followed by 30 minutes of Questions to the Prime Minister.

Next come Urgent Questions. These are only rarely allowed but, if they are, they only last 20 to 30 minutes. These are followed by Statements. There may be none but there is usually one, and often more then one, and each can last for up to forty-five minutes or an hour, much to the frustration of Ministers and their officials waiting for subsequent business. The first Statement on a Thursday is usually the Business Statement by the Leader of the House, who needs briefing on Early Day Motions.

Next (briefly) come applications to the Speaker for Standing Order 20 (i.e. Emergency) Debates. Applications are rarely accepted but, if they are, they take place later that day or next day. And then there might be a Ten Minute Rule Bill – an opportunity for an MP to speak for ten minutes on a topic which they regard as important. Another Member (but not a Minister) might reply, again for up to ten minutes.

And then at last we get to debates on Bills, Opposition motions and so on, which run through to a final 30 minute Adjournment Debate.

There can be considerable variations on the above – especially as Parliament is experimenting with different formats and timetables, including morning debates on non-contentious business in Westminster Hall. (Sittings actually take place in the Grand Committee Room just off Westminster Hall.) Your Parliamentary

Clerk will keep you right, and will give you the phone number of the police officer at the back of the Speaker's chair, where Ministers enter the chamber and where officials enter the box. He or she is unfailingly helpful and will in particular be able to tell you the time before which your business is unlikely to start, so allowing you to maximise your time in a nearby coffee bar or, if in the middle of a panic, in your office.

Parliamentary Questions

It cannot be stressed too strongly that Ministers and officials are under a duty to be both open and absolutely honest when answering questions from parliamentarians, whether at question time, in debate or in correspondence. Put simply, MPs are entitled to straight answers to straight questions.

Written Questions are those where both the question and answer are written, and they are part of the process by which MPs gather information from the Government. They tend not to be used for political point scoring because they do not usually receive much media attention. Therefore, unless the question is obviously antagonistic, Ministers will usually reject draft answers which are deliberately cagey.

In general, it is best to aim for accuracy and brevity in both the draft reply and the background note. And if the reply is likely to fill more than two columns of *Hansard*, you might suggest that the answer is that 'I will write to the Hon. Member and will place a copy of my letter in the Library'.

On the other hand, Parliament is a political arena and indeed some Parliamentary 'questions' – and especially Oral Questions – in substance amount to little more than political point-scoring. Therefore, as noted earlier, it is perfectly proper for a civil servant to prepare a draft letter, Statement or Parliamentary Answer which praises the Government's policies, and it is perfectly proper for our drafts to omit facts and arguments which might cast doubt on the appropriateness of those policies. But even in these circumstances, any factual element to the answer has to be accurate and the answer, when read as a whole, must not mislead the reader.

The more pedantic of my colleagues will wish me to point out that Oral Questions are actually written, in the sense that they appear on the Order Paper and are not repeated before the Minister rises to reply to them on the floor of the House. But the answers are oral, as are Supplementary Questions and their answers. There are therefore two stages to preparing answers to Oral Questions. First there is the easy bit, drafting a short answer to the Question as tabled. Second, and much harder, you have to anticipate what lies behind the Question by suggesting key points to make and answers to possible Supplementaries.

Prime Minister's Questions are almost always open questions about the PM's engagements, so allowing the questioner to ask Supplementaries about any issue which is causing controversy. You should therefore offer briefing (via Parliamentary Branch) if your subject has become newsworthy, providing only one or two key points to make, so that the Prime Minister can forcefully and succinctly deal with any attack. Do not provide politicised material. This will be done by your Special Adviser and staff in Number 10. And you should provide only as much defensive material as is necessary to keep the Prime Minister from making a serious mistake.

In dealing with all Parliamentary Questions (PQs), you should remember that the Ministerial Code makes it very clear that Ministers must not knowingly mislead Parliament or the public, and should be as open as possible with Parliament and the public, withholding information only when disclosure would not be in the public interest, which should be decided in accordance with any relevant statute law and current Open Government law and practice. Ministers also have a duty to give Parliament and the public as full information as possible about the policies, decisions and actions of the Government. It is our responsibility to help Ministers fulfil these obligations, and information should never be omitted from a draft reply simply because its disclosure could lead to political embarrassment or administrative inconvenience. But of course potential problems should be highlighted when the draft reply is submitted to the Minister.

It is different, of course, if the requested information is classified, or has been given in personal or business confidence. Ministers should be advised to refuse to answer any question which calls for such information, on the grounds of commercial confidentiality etc. An MP will sometimes, inadvertently or deliberately, show interest in an issue, the full exposure of which would be seriously damaging to the nation or to one or more individuals or businesses. In these circumstances it is sometimes possible for a Minister to meet the MP in question and explain the need for discretion – for the time being at least. If necessary, there can be consultation on 'Privy Council terms' between a Cabinet Minister and a senior member of the Opposition.

It can be interesting to debate whether honesty is required in certain hypothetical situations. But these circumstances are very unlikely to apply to any of us at any time in our career. In short, therefore, Ministers must always be given answers which are neither dishonest nor misleading. It is not clever to do something else; it is unprofessional and wrong.

Urgent Questions

Your job is to prepare clear briefing for the Speaker so that he or she can decide whether the Question should be allowed. The briefing usually has to be prepared in a great hurry (Urgent Questions can be tabled up to midday on Mondays and 10.00 am on other days), and the Speaker likes to be briefed by midday, so time can get ridiculously short). The briefing should therefore be very short and essentially factual, containing (if appropriate) enough information to demonstrate that the matter has already been well aired, or that the matter is not urgent, or that it is not the direct responsibility of the Government. Indeed, if it looks as though an Urgent Question might well be allowed, Ministers will often volunteer a Statement (see below) so as to avoid appearing to be forced into answering to the House.

You will know within a few minutes whether the question has been allowed. If it has then you will need to move very quickly to prepare your Minister for the 20 to 25 minute session beginning after Oral PQs.

Standing Order 20 (Emergency) Debates

Your role is to provide briefing so that the Speaker can decide whether to hear the application for an emergency debate, and if the application is heard, whether to accept the request. The MP's application can take up to only three minutes. If the application is successful, you will have to prepare for a full-scale debate either that evening or (you hope) the next day.

Early Day Motions

These statements of opinion signed by MPs are seldom debated, but you will need to brief the Leader of the House on them. And if the Opposition Front Bench table an EDM contrary to Government policy, you will quickly have to draft an amendment.

Ministerial Statements

Statements are normally made about major issues and developments which are likely to attract much attention both in Parliament and in the media. They are major events and take high priority. The word 'Statement' is a little misleading in that the Statement itself (which is read out by the Minister – and almost always a Cabinet Minister) is always followed by a grilling by interested MPs from both sides of the House. The Statement itself therefore needs to be drafted with great care so as to ensure that it is clear, informative and concise, and contains no hostages to fortune. The Minister's Private Office will clear the draft with Number 10 and a copy of the Statement is then usually given to the Opposition 15-30 minutes before it is due to be made. A Lords Minister will usually repeat the Statement in the House of Lords. As well as drafting the Statement, you will need to prepare thorough briefing for the Supplementary Questions in both houses.

By the way, if your Minister wants or needs to make an announcement that does not justify a Statement, you should consult your Parliamentary Branch about tabling a Written Ministerial Statement. Copies are then made available next day in the Vote Office, and the Statement also appears in *Hansard*.

Adjournment Debates

These daily debates allow MPs to draw attention to constituency and other matters. It is often the case that there are no other MPs in the Chamber, and the Minister will usually wish to respond sympathetically to what is said. You will need to provide a closing speech (about 10 minutes' worth) which the Minister will amend or embroider once he or she has heard the opening speech, and you will need to supply background briefing.

At least one official will need to be in 'the box', and if you miss your last train then the Private Office will arrange to get you home. However, if the debate is likely to be in the small hours, and the Minister is familiar with the subject, you might be let off!

Timed adjournment debates also take place on the last day of each Parliamentary term. Eight topics are selected by ballot at least two days beforehand and the debates are otherwise broadly similar to the daily debates.

House of Lords Business

Procedures in the House of Lords are broadly similar to those in the Commons, but they vary considerably in matters of detail. For instance, I can never remember the difference between starred and unstarred questions. So don't assume anything but check with the Private Secretary to the Minister concerned, and double-check with Parliamentary Branch. If the two of them agree then you have probably been given accurate information. If they disagree, then get them to sort it out!

Generally, of course, the Lords are much more civilised than the Commons, and you get much more notice of most business. But do not underestimate the Lords. Many of them are real experts, and many of them are very experienced politicians. Also government spokesmen and women in the Lords have wider portfolios than their counterparts in the Commons. These two factors together mean that your drafting and briefing has to be of very high quality.

Bills and Standing Committees

Bills (i.e. draft legislation) go through a number of stages, in the following order.

- Your Minister gets policy approval and drafting authority from Cabinet colleagues. This means that Parliamentary Counsel can start work, having been instructed by your departmental solicitor who is in turn instructed by you.

- Your Minister then gains collective agreement that the Bill will form part of the legislative programme and (unless it is relatively minor and uncontroversial) it is announced in the Queen's Speech in November.
- There then follows Introduction and First Reading (usually a formality).
- Second Reading then triggers a major debate on the merits of the Bill.
- Committee Stage follows, in which a Standing Committee examines the legislation in great detail. (Committees of the Whole House are used for the Committee Stage of certain major Bills, particularly on constitutional matters.)
- Next comes Report Stage, in which the Bill as amended in Committee is reported back to the Whole House, and again debated, and possibly further amended.
- Finally, for the moment at least, there comes Third Reading, following which the Bill is approved for onward transmission to the Lords (if it began in the Commons) or to the Commons (if it began in the Lords).

Then the whole process is repeated in the other House. If the Bill has not been amended in the other House then it goes on to the Monarch for Royal Assent, whereupon it becomes law. If it has been amended then it ping-pongs between the two Houses until they agree on a text, whereupon it then goes forward for Royal Assent.

It will be clear from the above that taking a Bill through Parliament is a major and high profile task, always entrusted to a separate Bill Team. If you get anywhere near this process, you must start by reading the detailed information and instructions which your department will make available to you. You should also go to see, and listen carefully to advice from, the Cabinet Secretariat and your Parliamentary Clerk. And take care that you have enough resources, in the form of people and PCs, photocopiers etc. The workload can be huge and urgent, especially during Committee Stage.

Select and Grand Committees

Select Committees oversee the work of individual departments, and sometimes call officials to give evidence. There are also some specialised Select Committees, such as the Public Accounts Committee and the European Scrutiny Committee.

The Scottish, Welsh and Northern Irish Grand Committees operate along similar lines except that, interestingly, they frequently hold meetings in Scotland etc.

Select Committees are appointed for a whole Parliament and so become experts on their subject matter. Party differences therefore tend to become less important as the months go by, and there is usually a good deal of consensus. Select Committees therefore deserve considerable respect.

Having decided what subjects it will look at, a Committee will generally call for written evidence from outsiders, and a position paper from the department. It will then take written and oral evidence before preparing a report for the Whole House. These are important documents to which Ministers are expected to respond in writing.

If you are asked to prepare evidence for, or brief a colleague who is to appear, or appear yourself, before a Select Committee then you should carefully read all the guidance that is available from your Finance Division and your Parliamentary Branch. If you or a fellow official is giving evidence then your Minister will require you to follow 'the Osmotherly Rules'. These are contained in a document entitled Departmental Evidence and Response to Select Committees, a copy of which you should obtain. Put shortly, you may describe and explain the reasons which caused Ministers to adopt existing policies but you should not give information which undermines collective responsibility or get into a discussion about alternative policies. In particular, you are not allowed to divulge:

- advice given to Ministers by officials;
- information about interdepartmental exchanges on policy issues, the level at which decisions were taken, or the manner in which Ministers consulted their colleagues;
- the private affairs of individuals, including constituents;
- sensitive commercial or economic information;
- information about negotiations with other governments or bodies such as the European Commission.

The Clerk to the Committee will usually give you a good idea of what is needed (if you are preparing a memorandum) and will try to predict the likely line of questioning (if you are appearing in person). The key things to remember are:

- be brief;
- be as helpful as you possibly can;
- be truthful and accurate, and say if you do not know the answer. (Correct any mistakes or misleading answers as soon as possible afterwards. This is often necessary, and Committees understand that mistakes are made under pressure).
- be tactful about having greater knowledge than the committee (if you do!);

- maintain self-control, even under provocation;
- do not tell jokes;
- you appear on behalf of your Minister who must agree your proposed response;
- your Minster is responsible for what information is given to the committee and for defending his or her decision as necessary;
- you may not publish written evidence – it belongs to the Committee;
- you may publish your response to a Committee report, but only after it has been received by the Committee.

Parliamentary Control of Expenditure

Students of history will recall that the Commons' control over the Crown, and subsequently over the Executive, was exercised through control over expenditure. This control is still jealously safeguarded by MPs, including through the Public Accounts Committee, to which 'Accounting Officers' (usually Permanent Secretaries) are directly accountable for the propriety and value for money of the department's expenditure. Civil servants may therefore only spend money if they comply with statutory constraints and detailed rules which are not found in the private sector and which can sometimes seem irksome and frustrating. In particular, it is always necessary to ensure that expenditure is permitted by, and within the limits set by, both the Treasury and Finance Division. It is absolutely wrong, and a serious disciplinary offence, to break or circumvent these expenditure controls.

In addition, MPs are understandably concerned to ensure that both Ministers and civil servants do not waste or profit from the taxes that are extracted from their constituents – many of whom are not well off and who would rightly object if civil servants either wasted their money or used it to fund an extravagant lifestyle, whether on or off duty. Put bluntly, those who want to be generously paid, or to operate a generous expense account, should not become civil servants.

The Public Accounts Committee, in particular, is quite properly intolerant of wasteful expenditure, and of decisions which cannot be supported by careful evaluation and comparison. The committee deliberates with the benefit of hindsight, and can therefore seem intolerant of risk-taking, and of the need to negotiate in uncertain conditions and against tight deadlines. The correct response is not to become risk-averse, but rather to ensure that the reasons for important decisions are properly documented, and supported by appropriate professional advice. With a little planning, this can be done even if the decision in question needs to be taken against a very tight deadline. Do not be surprised if a failure to take these elementary precautions is regarded with considerable suspicion by both the PAC and other observers.

6 Integrity, Honesty, Impartiality and Objectivity

The Civil Service Code

The Civil Service Code summarises the constitutional framework within which all civil servants work. It is such an important document that it is worth reproducing its key elements here:

> *The constitutional and practical role of the Civil Service is, with integrity, honesty, impartiality and objectivity, to assist the duly constituted Government whatever its political complexion, in formulating their policies, carrying out decisions and in administering public services for which they are responsible.*
>
> *Civil servants should conduct themselves with integrity, impartiality and honesty. They should give honest and impartial advice to the Minister without fear or favour, and make all information relevant to a decision available to them. They should not deceive or knowingly mislead Ministers, Parliament, or the public.*

Civil servants should endeavour to deal with the affairs of the public sympathetically, efficiently, promptly and without bias or maladministration.

Civil servants should endeavour to ensure the proper, effective and efficient use of public money.

Civil servants should not misuse their official position or information acquired in the course of their official duties to further their private interests or those of others. They should not receive benefits of any kind from a third party which might reasonably be seen to compromise their personal judgement or integrity.

Civil servants should conduct themselves in such a way as to deserve and retain the confidence of Ministers or Assembly Secretaries and the National Assembly as a body, and to be able to establish the same relationship with those whom they may be required to serve in some future Administration. They should comply with restrictions on their political activities.

Civil servants should not without authority disclose official information which has been communicated in confidence within the Administration, or received in confidence from others. They should not seek to frustrate or influence the policies, decisions or actions of Ministers, Assembly Secretaries or the National Assembly as a body by the unauthorised, improper or premature disclosure outside the Administration of any information to which they have had access as civil servants.

The rest of this chapter examines the practical implications of these rules. It also looks at other aspects of our professional environment, such as judicial review, human rights, freedom of information, and devolution.

Political Impartiality

The civil service is required to be politically impartial, and able loyally and with equal commitment to serve Governments of all political persuasions. This means that:

- you may not publicly defend the decisions and views of your Ministers (as distinct from explaining them), including by writing to newspapers;
- you must even avoid saying or writing anything which could be quoted as demonstrating that you personally (or your colleagues) either agree or disagree with Ministers' decisions;
- you may not disclose the advice that you have given to Ministers;

but on the other hand

- you must explain and implement your Minister's policies with real commitment, whatever your personal views.

It can be very hard to follow the above advice, especially when a Minister or Special Adviser does not share your view of the borderline between 'explaining' a policy and 'defending' it. It is even more difficult if you strongly support – or strongly object to – decisions that have been made, or might be made, by Ministers. It is not always possible to hide those views from colleagues, and it is sometimes difficult to hide them from those outside the Government with whom you come into frequent contact. But it is absolutely essential that you give no sign that you oppose the principles and underlying thrust of the Government's policies, nor must you suggest that you do not respect your Minister.

It can be even more difficult to follow the above advice where minor decisions are concerned. ('Of course I will try to get him to open your conference. It's an important occasion'). But you will learn from bitter experience that the advice is sensible, for it is embarrassing all round when the Minister refuses to do what you suggest. There is, I am afraid, no alternative to sounding rather pathetic and merely promising that the case will be put to the Minister, adding that you cannot predict the result. Quite simply, it should never be possible for anyone to be able to criticise Ministers for failing to take your advice. And it is even more important that incoming Ministers should be unaware of the extent or otherwise of your personal support for their predecessors' policies.

Equally, you may not be asked to engage in activities which call into question your political impartiality, or which give rise to criticism that people paid from public funds are being used for party political purposes. You may not, of course, engage in political activities. And you may not help draft 'Dear Colleague' letters unless they are to be sent to all MPs. You are, however, allowed to provide Ministers with facts which might be used in political speeches etc., and you are allowed to check Ministers' political speeches for factual accuracy. You are also allowed to comment on the analysis, costings and proposals contained in documents produced by political organisations, including the Opposition, but you must not draft Ministers' responses to such documents.

You may not brief an MP (including from the Government party) or agree that an MP may visit a Government office etc. without Ministerial approval. Ministers will usually agree to factual or uncontroversial briefings and visits, but they sometimes want to get involved themselves, in which case any meeting or visit has to be arranged at a time convenient for both the Minister and the MP.

Equality of Treatment

The public expect both Ministers and their officials to deal equally with everyone, and with every organisation, without prejudice, favour or disfavour. This simple but vital concept has a number of useful consequences.

First, it enables you to ask appropriate questions, however grand the person or organisation with which you are dealing. For instance, an enquiry into the financial standing of a multinational can often be less rigorous than a similar enquiry of a small firm. But large firms can go bust, so you should never take anything for granted. Ask a carefully targeted question and then decide whether further questions are necessary. Take particular care if you have heard a critical rumour or comment. There can be smoke without fire, but the two are usually closely associated.

Second, it is your defence against the senior or public figure who might otherwise expect you to give them priority, or rubber stamp some sort of application. You must never allow queue-jumping, nor must you ever refrain from asking a pertinent question, whoever you are dealing with. (It is of course perfectly reasonable to 'fast track' some work for a senior person who has a genuine need for it to be done quickly. But you must be sure that you would do the same for anyone else with a similar need, and that they are not jumping ahead of someone whose needs are just as great, but who is less well connected.)

Incidentally, the vast majority of senior/public figures understand perfectly well that they have to receive the same treatment as everyone else. If they get stroppy then (a) they believe that everyone should be receiving better treatment (if they are right then you should improve the service to everyone), or (b) they are trying to hide something (never allow yourself to be bullied into dropping a potentially important line of questioning), or (c) they are simply pompous (in which case don't favour them, but don't set out to punish them either).

Third, it is your defence against anyone, including journalists, who might ask you to give them advice and information that you have not given to others. If possible, of course, you should be free with information But there are no circumstances in which you should give information or advice to one person that you would not give to anyone else that asked a similar question.

Oversight by the Courts

It almost goes without saying that the Government itself, and individual civil servants, must take particular care to obey the law. After all, if the law makers and their servants will not respect the law, why should anyone else? It follows that it is a very serious matter for an individual civil servant to be dishonest, whether in their private or public life.

It is equally important that we apply the utmost good faith in our official dealings with the judicial machine. If we become involved in a legal dispute, we have a duty to assist the court by drawing all appropriate facts and arguments to its attention. There can be no question of hiding or distorting evidence so as to improve the chances of 'success', even if it is felt that such tactics are being deployed by the other side.

Unlike the private sector, we are also subject to judge-made 'Administrative Law' in the form of Judicial Review (JR) of decisions made public bodies, including the Government. As one judge put it:

'Judicial review is about telling the powerful how to behave when they make decisions.' It is therefore a very dynamic part of the law, and decisions are greatly influenced by the judge's perception of whether the powerful have acted fairly (a very subjective concept) in all the circumstances. Future decisions are also likely to be influenced by human rights consideration. Every civil servant should therefore read *The Judge Over Your Shoulder* (www.treasury-solicitor.gov.uk/home_pages/docs/judge.pdf). And you should also consult a lawyer before you, or your Minister, makes any decision which might conceivably be challenged as being in some way unfair.

It is often said that JR is 'merely' all about process, but it is also true that good process will greatly increase the chances of your making a good decision, so JR has value if it persuades you not to cut corners. In addition, however, JR may be brought if there is any appearance of bias, or going beyond Parliamentary authority.

It follows that judges are not supposed to overturn a decision which appears to have been properly and fairly made (even if they personally disagree with it). However, the Courts will intervene 'if no reasonable Minister properly directing himself could have reached the impugned decision'. Although this is a stiff test, decisions are in practice quashed more often than you would expect. So it is well worth stopping and considering whether your actions will appear fair and reasonable to a dispassionate observer well after the event.

Many applicants for Judicial Review claim that a Minister has taken 'irrelevant factors' into account when making a decision. Of course many decisions are essentially political in nature, e.g. the balance to be struck between the needs of the environment and the needs of the economy. Parliament has therefore provided that such decisions must ultimately be taken by or on behalf of Ministers. And Ministers are politicians, not judges. They are therefore expected, and allowed, to make those decisions against the backdrop of their political agenda. But they are not expected, or allowed, to make decisions in a way which is limited by that agenda. Therefore, when advising Ministers in these cases, you should divide the factors bearing on the decision into three classes:

A The first are those factors that are specified, in the appropriate legislation, as relevant to the decision. The decision has to be consistent with those factors. In other words, it should be possible to imagine a reasonable person taking a similar decision on the basis of the same facts, without taking into account other factors.

B Ministers may also take other relevant factors into account, such as the economic needs of a particular region, or the need to be seen to be encouraging competition.

C But Ministers may not take into account irrelevant factors such as the regional political situation, or recent political donations from the company in question.

The borderline between the categories can sometimes be indistinct. Legal advice should therefore be taken if you are in any doubt.

Human Rights

The Human Rights Act 1998 incorporates the European Convention on Human Rights into UK law. The Convention is a treaty of the Council of Europe which is based, along with the European Court of Human Rights, in Strasbourg. Neither body is part of the EU.

The Convention guarantees a number of rights and freedoms, including:

- the right to a fair and public trial within a reasonable time (this applies to any case involving civil rights and obligations, and not just criminal trials);
- the right to respect for private and family life, home and correspondence;
- the right to peaceful enjoyment of possessions and protection of property.

The Convention is intended, amongst other things, to promote the ideals and values of a democratic society. It is therefore to be given a broad and generous interpretation, and the courts will look at the substance and reality of what is involved, and not just the form. The Convention is also a dynamic document which must be interpreted in the light of present-day conditions. Societies and values change and these changes are taken into account.

The Convention incorporates two important concepts. The first is proportionality – any interference with a Convention right must be in proportion to the aim being pursued. The second concept is legal certainty. Any action impinging on a human right must be authorised by a specific legal rule or regime and not, for instance, by non-statutory guidance.

The Strasbourg Court looks to see whether there are common European standards but on the other hand it is reluctant to substitute its own views for those of domestic authorities in those cases where it is necessary to strike a balance between competing considerations. This applies, for instance, where there is a balance to be struck between the demands of the community or society and individual property rights. Nevertheless, the Court has, for instance, been very reluctant to permit the deprivation of property without compensation.

It is already clear that the Human Rights Act will fundamentally alter the way in which the British courts approach the interpretation of statutory provisions. In particular, they will strive to find a meaning which is compatible with the Convention, even if this involves finding a meaning which the words of the statute would not ordinarily bear. In doing so, the Courts can quash or ignore secondary legislation, but they cannot override the clear meaning of primary legislation, even though it may be equally clear that the legislation is incompatible with the Convention. The Courts will in these circumstances issue a declaration of incompatibility whereupon Parliament must decide whether it agrees with the Courts, and change the law, or whether it disagrees with the Courts and risk having the aggrieved citizen take the case to the European Court of Human Rights.

Freedom of Information

Civil servants working on the development of particular policies are not directly accountable to the public. However, the public are our ultimate paymaster and we should therefore be open with them, unless there is a very good reason not to be. After all, we deal with complex issues and have no monopoly of wisdom or knowledge. It therefore makes sense to explain the way in which the Government's policies are developing, before they are set in concrete, so that we can be told if we are getting anything wrong, and in particular if our assumptions are incorrect. We should also explain the way in which we administer our schemes and make decisions, and we should make available the internal guidance and rules which govern our procedures.

There have always been two important limits to the above approach. First, we have respected the needs of those who have provided us with information in confidence, or with commercially sensitive information. We should not disclose such information without the permission of the person who provided it. Second, we have not disclosed our advice to Ministers, for this weakens their position if they decide that they will not accept our advice. Open Government in this area would thus tend to increase the power of officials as compared with Ministers, and this is hardly in the interests of democracy. Similarly, there is a strict prohibition against revealing that the Law Officers have been consulted, let alone what they have advised.

In the past, if I have not been sure whether to provide information, I have asked myself whether we would provide it in response to a Parliamentary Question. If we would, then we should be prepared to give it without such a stimulus. But if we would refuse information to an MP, we should prima facie refuse to give it to the public.

More detailed advice is in the 1997 Code of Practice on Access to Government Information. And in future, of course, the test will be that laid down in the Freedom of Information Act 2000, which comes into force in January 2005.

In general, the Act follows the approach described above, and establishes a general right of access to information held by public bodies, subject to certain exemptions, including:

- information relating to the formulation or development of government policy;
- Ministerial communications;
- advice from the Law Officers – and requests for such advice;
- information whose disclosure would be likely to prejudice collective responsibility;
- information whose disclosure would constitute a breach of confidence;
- information whose disclosure would be likely to prejudice commercial interests.

It remains to be seen where the border will be drawn between exempt and non-exempt information, and there will no doubt be much debate about the definition of 'information relating to the formulation . . . of policy'. It will also be difficult to distinguish some facts from opinions or probabilities, and no doubt some departments will have problems with requests for certain types of information. However, if your general approach is to be open, and to respond positively to informal requests, then you will seldom if ever find yourself corresponding with the Information Commissioner. But if it begins to look as though you might be getting into a dispute in this area then make sure that you read the Act and the guidance material very carefully, and also consult experienced colleagues, including your department's Freedom of Information officer. I will also include up to date advice on the website which accompanies this book (www.civilservant.org.uk) But do bear in mind that, if you make a mistake, the public are more likely to see conspiracy than cock up, especially in the early days.

Recruitment and Promotion

Civil servants are also heavily constrained when they select individuals to fill particular posts. It is fairly easy to arrange a level transfer (i.e. without a significant pay rise) from one job to another. But you need to take great care when appointing someone from outside the civil service, or promoting someone from within it. The basic rules for these appointments are as follows:

- all such appointments must be made on the basis of fair and open competition;
- all prospective applicants must be given equal and reasonable access to adequate information about the job and its require-

ments, and about the selection process;

- all applicants must be considered equally on merit at each stage of the selection process;
- selection must be based on relevant criteria applied consistently to all the candidates;
- selection techniques must be reliable and guard against bias.

You cannot therefore appoint someone from outside the civil service to a job without an advertisement and competition, even if you believe them to be ideally or uniquely suitable. There are limited exceptions, such as for inward secondees, but you should take a close look at the relevant guidance before attempting to make use of such an exception.

And don't forget the need for high quality induction to follow any recruitment process. It is particularly important that new entrants to the profession are introduced to the Civil Service Code, and come to understand its importance and implications. There should be no question of local mission statements or departmental core values overriding the provisions of the code.

Conflicts of Interest

Great care needs to be taken to avoid conflicts of interest, whether real or perceived. You may be certain that you could rise above them, but others will doubt it. All potential conflicts of interest, including conflicts with the interests of your immediate family, must therefore be disclosed to managers, remembering that an innocuous friendship, investment, gift or treat can be transformed overnight into a possible conflict of interest. The following paragraphs provide guidance, but nothing in them should be taken to detract from departmental guidance, which should be consulted, and taken to prevail, in case of

doubt. Indeed, certain individual departments, or parts of departments, have additional requirements above those mentioned below.

Gifts, hospitality etc. may be divided into three categories.

First, there are gifts from a company whose services you are using or
might use, or with whom you might negotiate grant or other
support, or which might materially benefit from decisions with
which you might be involved. There are absolutely no circumstances
in which you can accept a gift of any value, or any hospitality more
substantial than a working lunch, from such a source. This prohibition extends to the use of Air Miles and other benefits offered by the
travel trade etc.

Second, expensive gifts (each departments defines its own limit) from
other donors must also generally be refused or returned.
Alternatively, it is sometimes possible to say to the donor 'Thank
you for the gift which I will use in the office rather than for my
personal use'. (You can donate wine to the Christmas party.) Failing
this, you can hand the gift over to the department, or pay the
department to let you keep it.

Third, any gifts, hospitality etc. whose acceptance is not prohibited
under the first two rules above, should also be refused unless the
acceptance can clearly be justified as contributing to the achievement
of your objectives. Put another way, the reason for the acceptance has
to be clearly defensible, always remembering the Greek proverb that
'gifts are poison'. Positive reasons for accepting hospitality include the
need to carry out an ambassadorial role, make contacts and gain
information. It is therefore generally OK to attend celebrations of a
company's success or longevity, or an industry-wide gathering,
including trade association dinners. It is also reasonable to accept

inexpensive gifts such as ties and pens, so as to avoid giving offence. Conversely, it is important to avoid developing a sense of obligation to a host or donor, and to avoid criticism (from those unable to benefit) of benefiting from lavish hospitality etc. In general, therefore, you should not accept tickets for major sporting events, Glyndebourne or Covent Garden. It is seldom a good argument that you are establishing or maintaining contacts at such events, because it is seldom appropriate or possible to discuss business. It is often useful to apply the 'wow' test. When you receive an invitation and find yourself saying 'wow' then it is time to refuse. A similar approach should be adopted when considering whether you might be accompanied by a partner to an event. Indeed, the negative factors can be more intense, given that the cost to the host will have doubled, and the opportunity to do business will have diminished. On the other hand, it can be helpful to be accompanied by a partner to an event at which one is trying to build up a relationship with the host or to an event at which one is acting as an ambassador, for instance at a company celebration or an event in aid of charity.

It is usually acceptable to accept local transport, lunch and refreshments when visiting private sector companies. But you may never let a private sector company pay your rail fare, air fare or overnight hotel bill. It is also acceptable to accept overnight accommodation in a company's guest house provided for that purpose, but of course you must not then claim overnight subsistence. And it is permissible to accept a free flight in a company plane if there is no convenient public transport and if the plane would have been making the journey anyway. But the offer of such transport should be refused if convenient public transport is available, or if the provision of the flight would cause the company to incur significant expense.

Financial Interests

We must all take particular care to avoid profiting, or enabling others to profit, (or even getting into a position where we could do these things) from information which is supplied to us in confidence. In particular, you must consult your line manager if you are asked to handle papers concerning any company (including a bank) in which you have invested, or with which you have any financial link. (However, standard bank accounts may be ignored for this purpose, unless they contain a huge amount of money.) You must also tell your manager if you hold shares in, or have any other link with, any company which is dealt with by you or your colleagues. You must do this immediately on joining the team, or immediately on acquiring the shares etc. This applies even if the shares are held via a PEP or ISA. Holdings in collective vehicles such as unit trusts need not be reported unless you have a large holding (over £1000) and you know that your trust has invested in a company or companies with which you are dealing.

You must also tell your line manager about any other employment or self-employment. And you must disclose links to all other bodies (including charities) if it looks as though you might be asked to deal with them on behalf of the department.

There are also strict rules about business appointments after retirement. It is obviously important that there should be no cause for any suspicion of impropriety when you take up a new job after retirement. All offers of employment should therefore be reported to your department who will if necessary involve the Advisory Committee on Business Appointments which gives advice on applications at the most senior levels, and reviews a wider sample in order to ensure consistency and effectiveness.

Devolution

Devolution raises many fascinating questions and problems but, in truth, most of them are mainly of interest only to academics and constitutional specialists. There is no reason why most of us should not retain sensible, non-adversarial relations with colleagues working for the devolved bodies.

The key thing, of course, is to show respect for countries which are proud of their national structures, institutions and industries, and of the ways in which they are very different from England. It is a mistake to worry too much if they take decisions which are different from those taken by Westminster. Diversity is not an unintended consequence of devolution. It is the whole point of it.

The relationship should also be entirely co-operative, and based on free and effective communication. If it would be helpful to share information on a confidential basis, you should not hesitate to do so, as long as the confidentiality is made clear to your colleagues – and as long as the information is exempt from disclosure under the Freedom of Information Act. Tensions will no doubt arise – for instance where, say, the Scottish interest in an EU negotiation is not the same as the wider UK interest. But these problems will be reduced, not exacerbated, by clear and open communication.

Open and effective communication also ensures that colleagues are not surprised by Whitehall announcements, followed as they always are by questions such as 'What are you doing on this in Wales?' Colleagues can respond constructively, even if they are pursuing different policies, as long as they have prior warning.

Above all, you must not be patronising. You should ask whether a devolved administration wishes to act in a certain way, and not suggest that they should do so or, even worse, tell them to do so. And remember that, although the UK Parliament retains the authority to legislate on any issue, whether devolved or not, the convention is that

Westminster will not normally legislate with regard to devolved matters in Scotland without the consent of the Scottish Parliament. This convention does not apply to incidental or consequential changes to Scottish Law where the purpose of the new law is reserved to the UK Parliament, but there should always be close consultation with Scottish colleagues, whatever the constitutional position.

As always, of course, look at more detailed and formal documents, including the formal Concordats with the devolved administrations, and consult experienced colleagues, if it looks as though a serious problem might be developing.

By the way, it is important to understand the respective roles of the post-devolution institutions. The Scotland Office, the Wales Office and the Northern Ireland Office are London-based departments headed by Secretaries of State who are members of the UK Cabinet. The Scottish Executive, the National Assembly for Wales and the various Northern Irish Departments are the executive bodies that report to Ministers elected by the Scottish Parliament and the Welsh and Northern Irish Assemblies.

Note particularly the constitution of the National Assembly for Wales. Unlike its counterparts in Scotland and Wales, the deliberative/legislative body and the executive are together legally one body. The problems that this created have been mitigated by drawing an internal dividing line. The deliberative/legislative Assembly is now organised through the Office of the Presiding Officer (OPO) whilst the executive now styles itself the Welsh Assembly Government.

General Elections

Parliament is usually dissolved two or three days after the Prime Minister announces the date of the election. If the Opposition agree, this allows the completion of important legislation, such as Finance Bills.

MPs cease to be MPs when Parliament is dissolved. Strictly speaking, therefore, all candidates are thereafter on an equal footing. But it is regarded as courteous for Ministers themselves to reply to letters written by MPs before the dissolution, or by former MPs after the dissolution. Private Secretary replies are normally sent to candidates (Government or Opposition) who were not members before the dissolution.

Ministers retain their appointments, usually through to the day after the election when the Prime Minister is ready to begin to appoint the new Government.

During the General Election period, the Government retains its responsibility to govern and Ministers remain in charge of their departments. Essential business must be carried on, but it is customary for Ministers to observe discretion as to initiating any new action of a continuing or long-term nature. Ministers usually try to avoid official engagements because they want to devote the time to campaigning. But they are free to undertake engagements they regard as important, although they should seek to avoid giving the impression that they are using such occasions for party political purposes. Similarly, attendance at some international meetings remains necessary. However, before undertaking to fulfil international commitments, Ministers should consider whether the subject matter is such that they can speak with the authority proper to a representative of Her Majesty's Government.

So far as the handling of correspondence is concerned, the general rule is that citizens' individual interests should not be prejudiced by the calling of an election. It follows that letters relating to them should be replied to, whether by Ministers or by officials on their behalf. But remember that correspondence may become public knowledge and might be used for political purposes. Replies to letters should therefore be as straightforward as possible, should avoid controversy, and, if to a candidate, should not distinguish between candidates of different parties.

All public appointments which might be regarded as politically sensitive should be frozen until after the election and, although routine information activities (i.e. the provision of factual information) continue during the election campaign, other information activities generally cease entirely.

7   Innovation

The next three chapters of this book deal with issues at the heart of
the delivery agenda, but they are also areas where civil servants face
similar problems to many of their private and voluntary sector
counterparts. In particular, why are we not more innovative? And
how do we become better leaders and managers? In response, I offer
the following advice, often taken from best practice in the private
sector.

I begin with some thoughts in response to persistent criticism that
the civil service too often fails to offer innovative solutions to policy
problems. In order to tackle this problem, it is first necessary to
understand the principal reasons why innovation might be difficult.
Most analysts come up with variations on the following six key
problems:

1 We work for politicians who in turn work in an adversarial and
   confrontational environment, under constant media scrutiny. It
   is the duty of the Opposition to oppose. New ideas are swiftly
   attacked, improvements are regarded as evidence of past failure,
   debates about the merits of particular proposals are seized upon
   as signs of divisions within Government, and mistakes are merci-
   lessly exposed and criticised. Ministers do not like to be
   out-shone by exciting, achieving and innovative officials, and do
   not thank us for exposing them to criticism for some new idea
   which has not yet been properly thought through. Any poten-

tially controversial idea which cannot be kept entirely secret is therefore best left well alone.

2   We are part of a profession, and cannot afford to alienate colleagues with whom we might have to work very closely for years to come. Also, our professional and financial rewards come mainly via promotion. It is therefore crucially important that we do not do anything which might upset a senior colleague, and in particular our manager and our Permanent Secretary. We therefore: do not encourage internal challenge; hesitate before saying anything which might be construed as foolish by any senior colleague – most of whom will be older than us; and are reluctant to draw attention to colleagues, or parts of a department, who are performing badly – and yet this is often a necessary pre-cursor to real change.

3   We work within quite distinct Government departments, with quite distinct budgets and for Ministers who are usually in competition with their colleagues in other departments. We develop a loyalty to the organisation, to our staff, to our budget and to our Ministers, which tends to inhibit free thinking.

4   It is a firm rule that the Treasury have to be consulted before we commit resources to anything 'novel or contentious'. And if that doesn't deter us, a colleague will soon remind us that our Permanent Secretary is directly accountable to Parliament for the way in which we spend public money. Mere suspicion that we might cause the Permanent Secretary to be asked questions will cause our judgement to be questioned.

5   Common sense, bolstered by the doctrine of collective responsibility, means that it is necessary to consult, often quite widely, before becoming committed to any significant new policy. Colleagues will inevitably express various concerns and, although

it might be possible to address each of them, the effort of doing so can be quite daunting.

6 Our work is dominated by major and apparently unquestionable policies, including those in manifestos. There are therefore significant limits to the extent to which we are permitted to think the unthinkable.

Against the above, let me make four important points.

1 Other organisations find it equally difficult to foster internal challenge and innovation. Indeed, variations on all the above problems, apart perhaps from the first and fourth, can be found in most other large professions and organisations.

2 There is nothing in our two key professional duties (to give independent, balanced advice, and to implement Ministers' decisions, even if we have advised against them) which stops us being innovative.

3 There is no suggestion that we should all become innovative or creative all the time. But those of us that are innovative – and when we are innovative – need to operate in a supportive environment.

4 Being innovative is not the same as being entrepreneurial. Whatever they may say, no-one, and least of all our Ministers, want us to treat public money as if it were our own, or do deals other than within clearly established boundaries.

I believe that there are lots of things we can do to overcome obstacles to innovation, including:

• planning,
• tackling departmentalitis,

- overcoming the fear of risk,
- working effectively with the media,
- encouraging our teams to be innovative.

Planning

The first thing to do, once you have a bright idea, is to decide the extent of the likely opposition and plan a strategy for overcoming it. (Detailed advice on taking a policy initiative through Whitehall can be found earlier in this book.) Don't be reassured by Ministers' and senior colleagues' well-meant protestations that they adore innovative and risk-taking officials. In practice, innovation is fine if there is relatively little political interest in the activity. It is also easier to innovate if you are working closely with customers, and responding to clear customer pressure. That is why colleagues in many agencies and local offices find it relatively easy to innovate, if they are not held back by their head offices. In contrast, just imagine the obstacles that would face the Prison Service in the unlikely event that they found a way of halving the recidivism rate, but at the cost of doubling the number of escapes. They would have to plan their innovation strategy very carefully, enlisting strong Ministerial support, gaining buy-in within the wider Service (which would take time), and – above all – becoming very innovative in managing their relationship with the media.

Departmentalitis

The strongest opposition will of course come from other departments, fuelled by departmentalitis. Gerald Kaufman MP has drawn attention to this debilitating Ministerial disease in his excellent book *How to be a Minister*.

*If you contract departmentalitis you will ruthlessly pursue your
own department's interests even if another department has a
better case: quite simply, your department must win . . . you
will forget that you are part of a government, that the fortunes
of the government are more important than the fortunes of your
own department.*

But the disease is also endemic amongst officials. We kid ourselves
that we run a finely-tuned machine, co-ordinating and consulting
effectively with colleagues elsewhere in Government. The truth is
that large groups – and indeed whole departments – all too often
compete with one another with the result that progress is too slow
and we make too many mistakes. As a result, the whole system can
begin to break down, and can sometimes break down completely.

The correct treatment for this disease is to refuse to play our cards
close to our chest, and refuse to seek power by failing to share information. Remember in particular that Ministers may not order us
not to consult or give relevant information to colleagues who have a
right to be consulted or to know what is going on. It is of course
sometimes sensible to work up a proposal before showing it to
colleagues. But you may not collude in a 'bounce' and if you feel
that colleagues in another department would expect to be told about
a proposal, then you must tell them. Officials in different departments should also try very hard to resolve differences without
involving Ministers. It is stupid and inefficient to conduct an
argument between officials through Ministerial correspondence.
This should be reserved for genuine debate between Ministers.

Of course it is no bad thing to become emotionally committed to
achieving your, or your Minister's, objectives, as long as you remain
politically impartial, well-balanced and professional. But you should
not set out to browbeat colleagues by arguing as if your preference

is self-evidently optimal. Such certainty can sometimes impress colleagues, and can sometimes sway decisions. But it is unprofessional and leads to decisions which are not soundly based. If your Minister's view does not seem to stand up to critical onslaught, you need to go back and discuss the problem. You should not simply try to bulldoze his or her view through.

And we should not hesitate to seek help from colleagues, even at the risk of appearing a little silly. Colleagues collectively have a wealth of knowledge and experience. Even if the problem is quite novel, they will have ideas about how you might tackle it. Indeed, most problems melt away if you simply seek help from colleagues. Almost everyone is more than willing to help, if they are approached in the right way. Indeed, it is often a very good idea to brainstorm an issue or to think aloud. But you should flag up very clearly that this is what you are doing, or else colleagues will think that you are delivering a considered view, and will not be impressed by your more hair-brained ideas!

You may occasionally come across someone – perhaps in a central department or in an influential position elsewhere in your department – who will seem to give you a direct order which you are not happy to accept. Remember that they cannot do so. No official other than in your management chain can give you an order, even if they are in Number 10, in the Cabinet Office, or even in your solicitors' office. They can draw your attention to their Minister's views, or to established policy, or to the law, and you will usually wish to take careful note. But in the last resort you must be guided by your own professional opinion. If you were to follow their advice, and they were to turn out to have been wrong, you could not subsequently blame them. If they continue to press their case, and you remain unpersuaded, you should consult Ministers or (in the case of legal advice) your department's senior legal adviser.

Finally, a word about dealing with the Treasury and Foreign & Commonwealth Office (FCO). Officials from these two departments tend to wield more power than others. This derives from the status of their Ministers and, in the case of the Treasury, from the fact that they act as HMG's banker. But the nature of their work means that some of them have little first-hand experience of their subject, or of achieving change. They are therefore required to question your policies without being expected to know the underlying facts. As a result, a small minority of Treasury and FCO colleagues give the impression that they believe that other departments are not clever enough, are not critical enough and do not work hard enough. In practice it is not too difficult to prove them wrong, as long as you are indeed fully on top of your policy issues, and the associated facts. If they can ask a relevant question which flummoxes you, you have only yourself to blame. The vast majority of Treasury and FCO staff are in fact very professional, experienced in their fields and invaluable colleagues. You should therefore treat them as equals, and expect them to treat you likewise.

The Fear of Risk

Because Ministers are publicly accountable, they are understandably reluctant to make mistakes that might expose them to criticism, even if only with the benefit of hindsight. Their officials should therefore be aware of the risks associated with various courses of action. But you will never achieve anything if your principal career objective is never to make a mistake. You should therefore aim to be risk conscious rather than risk averse. It is helpful to think in terms of a spectrum of risk.

There will be high risk if the suggested action will commit a great deal of money or other resource; if the repercussions from the action are unpredictable; if there is a history of serious error in this area; if the decision is of significant political or media interest; if there will be many losers and/or if there will be a small number of heavy losers. If these features are present then do not rush the decision. You should consult and plan very carefully, and if possible test the water by piloting any new scheme or activity, so as to test its practicality in the real world. In other words: 'Don't bet the business'.

There is low risk if an error would have little cost, is unlikely, could easily be corrected and/or is of little political or media interest. In this case, do not delay and keep consultation to the absolute minimum. Get on with it! Far too many civil servants agonise at length over minor decisions, and rush the major ones. They obey the well known law that the time devoted to the decision is in inverse proportion to its importance. Feel free to break this particular law!

But there are many intermediate cases where decisions carry medium risk. In these cases you should ask 'why not?' rather than 'why?'. Try out the idea on one or two interested observers, without exhaustively arguing the pros and cons. If there is no strong opposition, then again get on with it without further consultation. Otherwise, think through the issue again – and especially those aspects which have concerned those you have consulted.

There is no need to worry all the time about possible Public Accounts Committee or media criticism of minor decisions. Such criticism is generally concentrated on major decisions where the risks were clearly high, and the spending or action clearly inappropriate. Indeed, Sir John Bourn, head of the National Audit Office, says: 'The problem is not that the Whitehall culture is risk averse .... Rather, it is risk ignorant. It takes the most fantastic risks without knowing it is doing so.' Therefore, as long as you are conscious of the scale of the risk associated with your decision, and prepared to justify your decision on that basis, whilst recognising that others might well have decided differently, you will not receive serious criticism. All this was neatly summarised by Sir David Omand who, when Permanent Secretary at the Home Office, told his colleagues: 'If you are not making mistakes, you are not trying hard enough'.

Dealing with the Media

Almost everybody gets almost all their information via the media. It is therefore vital, if you are to deliver your objectives, that your media relations are first class. Indeed, many parts of government are engaged in what amounts to a permanent campaign. There is also much truth in the saying that 'you should feed the media or else they will feed on you'. You should therefore make every effort to be proactive, open and honest with the media, who will often be grateful for a clear exposition of your objectives and activities.

But keep the following warnings in the front of your mind.

The first and overriding rule is that you must never, ever talk to the media without first talking to your press office – who will generally talk to journalists themselves, unless you are senior and properly trained and prepared.

Second, remember that we are not accountable to the media – nor are Ministers, though you sometimes wouldn't think so from the way in which parts of the media sometimes behave. There is no difference in principle between talking to a reporter and talking to any other member of the public. You should therefore not give information to a reporter that you would not give both to any other reporter and to any other member of the public.

Third, journalists do not trust you. They may be very polite, and they may like you, but they know that you represent Ministers, and they trust Ministers even less. Anyway, very few civil servants are any good at giving succinct information to those unfamiliar with the subject matter. All reporters have therefore had some experience of receiving over-optimistic predictions and over-rosy judgements (because Ministers and officials have a natural desire to paint themselves and their decisions in the best possible light), and over-simple, false or misleading information (because of misunderstandings arising from rapid oral communication).

Fourth, many in the national media seem to be interested in little other than entertaining their readers, and will use you, or your Ministers, for that purpose if they possibly can. Therefore, unless your story is very straightforward and/or you are very experienced, aim at essentially factual media such as local press, trade journals, the *Financial Times*, and radio and TV programmes aimed at business audiences.

It follows (see rule one!) that you should make sure you have access to first class advice – particularly from your department's press office, but often also from outside experts. This is not the place to repeat all the advice that your press office will give you, but some of the basics are as follows.

Don't waste effort. Don't issue boring irrelevant press notices or seek media attention for trivial stories. Do get a reputation for saying things that are worth listening to. If you need to put something on the record, use the web, or issue an information note, or maybe use a Written Ministerial Statement. Save press releases for genuinely interesting and newsworthy stories.

Keep the message simple – one main argument and a couple of supporting points. Press notices, for instance, should begin with the key points you want to get across:

- What is being planned, decided, opposed or supported?
- Why is it important?
- Where is it taking place?

- Who is doing it?
- When will it happen?
- How many people will it affect?
- How much will it cost?

If you can't distil 'the news' into a headline and one or two short supporting sentences, then don't bother with a press release. You should not use the media to communicate complex messages.

When you have worked out your message, make sure it is seen and understood by anyone who might come into contact with the media.

Make sure you have answers to all the questions that a journalist could sensibly ask. Key facts, and answers to all the most obvious questions, should go into any press notice. But you need to have a background 'Q & A' covering everything else for use by anyone who might possibly be asked about your subject. There is nothing worse than having different people giving different answers to the same question, and it's almost as bad if it appears, because of lack of preparation, that you have not thought about an important aspect of the issue.

You must never ever have any direct contact with the media unless (a) you are properly trained, (b) you are very experienced, (c) your press office have told you that they trust you and (d) the subject is neither novel nor contentious. Even then, a press officer will generally accompany you, or sit beside you when you are on the phone. If not, you must subsequently report what you have said.

If you are to be interviewed, here are some basic rules which you should follow:

- Clearly identify your role. Are you speaking as yourself (i.e. an expert on a particular issue) and only saying what you believe to be true and sensible? Or are you speaking on behalf of Ministers ('The Government believes' etc.). If the latter, consider yet again whether you should be doing the interview at all. You may not defend (as distinct from explain) government policies. Ministers should speak on their own behalf.

- Ensure that you can answer every conceivable question without prevarication.
- Prepare very carefully what you are going to say, keep it simple and do not stray beyond the area you have prepared.
- Try to 'answer and move on'. In other words, especially when being interviewed on the radio or TV, first answer the question but then add a comment or story which takes the interview in a direction which allows you to get your point across. You, not the interviewer, should be in control of what you say.
- Never knowingly lie or mislead.
- If you make a mistake, correct it as soon as possible.

Finally, when talking to a newspaper reporter, you should generally specify that you are talking 'for background'. He or she is not then supposed to indicate that they have been briefed by a civil servant. This is so that you can avoid upstaging your Ministers, and not because you are embarrassed by what you are doing or saying. (There is no point in asking to be 'off the record'. If you say anything interesting to a reporter, they are bound to report it – which is why you should never give to one reporter any information which you would not give to any member of the public.)

Creating Innovative Teams

Teams become innovative when they are well-led, truly empowered within clear boundaries, and measured by results. In addition, you have to encourage a little rebellion and a questioning culture. Allow people, if they wish, to squirrel away a little time to work on pet projects. Expose problems – otherwise they will not get solved – and reward innovation through pay and promotion as well as in less tangible ways. Do not create a team which is excessively harmonious, for this stifles innovation. These subjects are so important that I devote the next chapter to them, for I firmly believe that if staff feel free to challenge and innovate, then remarkable things will be achieved.

8   Leadership

Leadership is about who you are. Management is about what you do. Sir Michael Bichard, a former Permanent Secretary, draws a clear distinction between managers and leaders:

> *Managers who control their organisations effectively may enable them to survive. But it is the leaders who create a sense of purpose and direction and who analyse, anticipate and inspire.*

Strong leadership is therefore essential if your team is to be innovative, efficient and successful. And yet one of the minor mysteries of the modern world is why there are so few effective leaders – in both the public and private sectors – when there is so much advice available in so many different books and courses. They all say pretty much the same sort of thing, which is that leaders:

- have a remorseless iron determination to make things happen;
- have an unshakeable inner conviction;
- constantly promote the same message;
- are different;
- have at least one weakness;
- set an example;
- keep things simple;
- are a little theatrical;
- are committed to their team;

- give people the freedom to take their own decisions
- liberate;
- encourage;
- support;
- develop people and teams;
- are fair;
- are sensitive to people's feelings;
- are honest
- are physically strong, and
- take risks.

Simple, eh? And of course many civil servants have a good number of the above attributes. But my own observation, for what it is worth, is that too few senior civil servants are sufficiently remorseless, committed, and honest. Let me explain what I mean.

Remorselessness

The first and most important characteristic of a leader is remorselessness, which takes two forms.

First, leaders feel no remorse when they make mistakes, or when some innovation fails to work. They recognise that they are dealing with humans, not machines, and human behaviour is highly unpredictable. Remorse and guilt are understandable, but quite unnecessary, even if something does not work in the way you expected.

Second, leaders are remorseless (in the sense of relentless) because they know that every improvement will take two or three times as long as they expect it to. But they don't let this stop them. Instead, they keep plugging away and eventually they and their teams achieve levels of performance that others can only dream of.

Commitment

Different situations call for different styles of leadership. Sometimes decisions need to be made very quickly and obeyed without question. But leaders nowadays almost always need the consent of those that they lead. Management consultants Kouzes and Posner describe leadership as 'a reciprocal relationship between those who choose to lead and those who decide to follow,' Modern leaders therefore need to be a cross between an old-fashioned captain of a ship and someone who is running for office. It follows that newly appointed leaders should go out of their way to get themselves elected – i.e. respected by their teams – in the first few days after their appointment. This simple fact does not seem to be understood by many colleagues.

If you are to be elected leader then you must commit to the team, with all its strengths and weaknesses. This is particularly important in the civil service if only because you are unlikely to be around long enough to replace them. And the civil service is anyway so large that, by definition, it has to employ a cross-section of the population. Of course you do not need put up with mediocrity or laziness. But you cannot insist on surrounding yourself with energetic geniuses. Your task is to get the best out of those who work for you, without forever wishing yourself somewhere else.

How do you show your commitment? You should:

- be very visible;
- set a good example, including by complying with rules and standards that have been set for your team;
- champion the team e.g. by defending them against unfair criticism, but also
- respond to fair criticism, whether of you or your team, in particular by putting matters right and by ensuring that the problem does not recur.

This all seems very obvious, but a Grade 7 friend of mine told me that three weeks passed before his newly appointed Grade 5 boss got round to meeting him, and he had yet to meet his Grade 3 after six months in the job. So some colleagues still have something to learn about visibility, commitment and leadership.

Honesty

According to Lucy Kellaway in the *Financial Times*, a good leader knows exactly when to be straight, when to be economical with the truth, when to lay it on with a trowel, and when to dissemble. This is absolutely right, but most of us spend too much time dissembling and too little time being honest with our staff. In particular, we have to be honest in making it clear to staff that they are employed for no other reason than to help the leader achieve his or her objectives. However much they like working together, the team must be directed to achieving a common goal. Everyone is then much better directed and motivated. Those who skirt round this fundamental truth simply waste time and create confused expectations.

Effective leaders also give clear and honest feedback to their staff – not all the time, but frequently enough to be effective. Any sustained failure to give honest feedback to colleagues – and of course we have all failed to some extent, and regretted it – can only end in disappointment, confusion and demoralisation. Honest appraisal is also a necessary companion to empowerment. Once the manager has defined the job that is to be done, he or she should aim to keep out of the way and let his or her staff do what is expected of them. But there must be regular informal and formal appraisal to ensure that the work stays on track.

The formal appraisal system is no doubt a necessary evil but it must be supplemented by informal appraisal, perhaps along the lines summarised in the book The One Minute Manager. This suggests that managers should give immediate feedback whenever they see good or bad work. Unfortunately too many managers give immediate feedback which is either always positive (and therefore dishonest) or always negative (which is debilitating). Colleagues quickly learn to appreciate the honesty of the manager who gives both sorts of feedback.

Formal appraisal is delivered within a structured system over which individual mangers have only limited control. But it is worth making three important points.

First, the formal annual appraisal is essentially one-way communication. The process might begin with self-appraisal (although I have my doubts about the effectiveness of this approach) but it is essentially an opportunity for the appraiser to be honest about how the other person has appeared to them over the preceding period. The person being appraised might well feel that the appraiser is wrong, but that should lead to improved communication and other action in the next reporting period. There can be no question of the appraisal being 'agreed' by the person being appraised, or subject to any form of appeal.

It is sensible, however, to show draft appraisals to the person on whom you are reporting, for you might well have forgotten some achievement, or you might have expressed something in an upsetting way. But the report should nevertheless remain your honest assessment of the other person, in comparison to other civil servants.

Second, appraisals should lead to action, whether by way of improved communication between manager and managed, or changes to objectives and expectations, or further training and development.

Third, it is better if appraisals are supplemented by 'upward feedback' or even '360 degree feedback'. There are several good systems which facilitate these processes but it must be stressed that they are not the same as 'upward appraisal'. I certainly want to hear from my staff what messages I am communicating to them e.g. through my behaviour. But it is not for them to tell me whether I am doing a good job.

So is that it? Well not quite. Leaders also have certain duties, and the three most important are that they must:

- set the boundaries;
- set the culture, within which their team will operate,
- empower their staff.

Leaders therefore need to carry out a difficult balancing act. On the one hand they need to be obsessive about setting boundaries and establishing the right culture. On the other hand, they need to empower and support. Those who get it right can usually then stand back and watch their team achieve surprising results. Further detail follows . . .

Setting Boundaries

It is vitally important that leaders should establish the ethical, financial, legal and other boundaries within which their colleagues should work. Problems (and sometimes severe problems) arise when these are not explicit or, even worse, when senior managers appear not to respect those boundaries. It is particularly important that civil servants should operate within the ethical, financial and legal boundaries laid down by Parliament and it is odd, to say the least, that it is difficult to find a written statement of these. I hope that other parts of this book go some way to defining the ethical etc. boundaries of which I am aware. It follows that I require everyone who works with me to respect these boundaries and to require all their staff to do the same.

Many boundaries are cultural, rather than ethical, in the sense that leaders are responsible for establishing the parameters within which staff deal with each other, with customers, with work pressures and so on. There is more on this below, but it is worth noting that some staff will constantly test your boundaries and force your intervention when the boundaries are likely to be breached. These colleagues will accuse you of micro-management. Other staff will respect your boundaries, and get on with their jobs with very little intervention from yourself. But they may as a result worry that you are not interested in them or their work area. It is therefore important that you explain your approach, and reassure those who think you have taken empowerment just a little too far.

Establishing the Culture

Leaders set the tone of the organisation – even in small but important ways. For instance, I hope that any visitor to my office will find that we are open, informal and hospitable. We feel that it makes a real difference if we are friendly and polite to each other, and offer refreshments and other courtesies to visitors. We in particular welcome the opportunity to talk about our work, and our approach to our work, and welcome visits from colleagues from Embassies, from industrialists, from students and from teachers.

I also expect everyone to recognise their responsibility for the safety, health and well-being of themselves and all their colleagues. We take the alarm bells seriously, even if we suspect that they are a false alarm. We take seriously all reports of sexual harassment, racial or sexual discrimination, or bullying. We give unquestioning support to colleagues who express concern about safety, harassment or discrimination. Above all, we do not ask colleagues to work so hard that they become stressed or over-tired. This is not only unethical, but it leads to mistakes and misjudgements – which in turn create more pressure.

Next, I encourage everyone to be customer-focused, where our customers are defined as the immediate beneficiaries of particular pieces of work. If you are preparing a briefing, your customer is the person who will use it. If you are organising a meeting, your customers will be those who attend the meeting. Our customers should be the sole and decisive judge of the quality of our work. The test is not whether we think that our work meets the requirements of the customer, but whether the customer is satisfied.

This implies measurement. You cannot tell whether your customer is satisfied unless you have asked him or her in a structured way. It should become second nature that your plans and your day-to-day work are driven by the expressed needs of your customers.

Measurement in turn drives continuous improvement. You and your team should constantly be looking out for ways – usually quite small in themselves – in which you could improve the satisfaction of the customer, or do the job more efficiently or effectively. The cumulative effort of many small improvements can be very noticeable indeed. Conversely, a cumulative failure to improve will eventually and inevitably lead to your customers feeling dissatisfied with the service that you are providing. It follows that imitation is a virtue. If you hear of a good idea, or see something working well, you should not hesitate to copy it so as to improve the service that you are providing to your customers. And if you run out of ideas for improvements, you should benchmark your team against another team or organisation. You will probably be surprised at what you find.

Continuous improvement in turn requires a no fault culture. We assume that everyone is trying to do a good job, within the limits of their skills, training and experience. Management gurus often say that 'customers' complaints are jewels to be treasured'. This is a bit over the top for most of us, but it is certainly true that complaints should never be ignored, and a single complaint often represents the tip of an iceberg of unvoiced dissatisfaction. Quality conscious organisations are therefore usually obsessive about investigating and resolving customer complaints, whether from internal or external customers. And complaints should never be used as a stick with which to beat your staff or other colleagues. If mistakes are made, or if quality standards are not met, then the person involved should be given clearer instructions or better training, or attention must be given to the process that they were carrying out, or they may not be in an appropriate job. (This judgement should not be arrived at lightly, but neither should it be ducked. If necessary, the person must be moved to a job that they can do.)

Empowerment

Empowerment is often confused with delegation. Delegation often means no more than that the delegate is simply told what to do and how to do it. Empowerment is better because it allows the colleague to choose how best to achieve his or her objectives and targets. Leaders don't delegate. They empower.

But note that empowerment is not a close relation of anarchy. People work to clearly specified objectives and targets, which they may not vary without consulting their boss and/or customer. Also, as noted above, they must work within other constraints laid down by the manager, including appropriate professional standards, standard procedures, quality standards and financial constraints. You should help them gain experience by empowering them, monitoring their performance and acting to relax the constraints as soon as you can.

In particular, submissions, draft letters etc. should be prepared by the person, however junior, best equipped to prepare a first draft. If the issue is not novel or contentious, and the person is appropriately experienced and trained, then there should be no need for the work to be countersigned by anyone else. Two heads are however better than one if an issue is novel or contentious. A senior colleague who countersigns work in these circumstances should concentrate on the substance of the work, and the way it will appear to Ministers or the recipients of letters etc. They should pay relatively little attention to the detail, style or grammar of the work.

Work should also be countersigned if the action officer is being trained, or gaining experience. It is helpful in these circumstances if the countersigning officer pays attention both to the substance of the work and to the detail, style and grammar. The objective of this intervention should, however, be to train the colleague so that coun-tersignature is in due course not necessary.

Achieving Change

One other task often falls to leaders: the planning and imple-mentation of significant change. It is then important to remember the 5 Cs – the five elements of any organisation, none of which can be changed without simultaneously causing change in the others:

- capacity, i.e. resources, and in particular staff numbers;
- capability (or competence), i.e. staff skills, training, experience and motivation;
- communications, including not only communications whilst the

change programme is being implemented, but also new ways of communicating once the changes have been implemented;

- culture, new relationships, attitudes to innovation, reward structures etc.;
- constitution, i.e. organisational structure, reporting lines etc.

Any change process therefore needs to consider the inter-relationship between these five elements, and what all of them – not just one of them – will look like at the end of the process. For instance, downsizing or de-layering must be accompanied by changes in the other elements, including improved training, accepting more errors, improved team-working and improved rewards. A failure to tackle these issues will mean that the slimmed-down organisation will perform markedly less well and will probably then return to its former size when it is forced to recruit again to improve its performance.

It follows that it is very difficult to manage change successfully, which is why so many reform and change programmes are unsuccessful. Indeed, there is much to be said for opting instead for continuous improvement of existing processes and structures, if Ministers will be patient enough.

9   Management

Leadership and management are inseparable – the two sides of the same coin – and yet quite different. We have already seen that leadership is about who you are. Management is about what you do. Management is the process of getting the most of out the resources at your disposal, and in particular about the process of getting the most out of your staff. The first stage is to set good objectives.

Setting Objectives

Civil servants have traditionally drafted their own objectives or job plan. Indeed, this approach was enshrined in official guidance published in the 1980s. However, I find this very odd. It is surely axiomatic that managers should take responsibility for defining what jobs they want done, what sort of person they want to do them and what standard of performance is expected. This should be clearly set out in a document which draws as necessary on the department's and division's written objectives, and should in the first instance be drafted by the manager, not the managed. After all, who else but the manager can in the first instance say why a particular individual is employed within their team?

I also dislike job descriptions which are all about what people do ('I give policy advice . . .', 'I manage . . .') rather than what they are trying to achieve. The usual response, of course, is that things like the health of an industry, or of the population, are dependent upon so many variables that it is positively unfair to credit any one civil servant with their improvement. There is of course some truth in this but it is also true that a great deal of effort will be wasted unless it is directed towards an identifiable (even if distant) objective. Also, the adoption of challenging and worthwhile objectives leads quickly to innovation, team-working and other good practices.

Objectives should be 'SMART', i.e. Specific, Measurable, Agreed, Realistic and Time-dependent. And they should be kept simple and relevant to the person who owns them. For instance, few of us can cope with more than three tiers of Aims/Vision, Objectives and Targets. And whilst an objective of the Permanent Secretary of the Home Office might be to cut crime, or keep it to a certain figure, this would become part of the vision of more junior officials who might be responsible for the Police Pension Scheme. The important thing is that those in charge of the pension scheme should know that it needs to be so designed that it will attract and retain high calibre police officers (and that is their objective) in order that they might cut crime.

And if anyone has difficulty in identifying worthwhile objectives, as distinct from day to day targets and activities, it is helpful to ask what would change, or how they and their team would be missed, if they did not exist. I have yet to meet anyone who has, when challenged in this way, failed to justify their employment in terms of meaningful objectives.

But take care! Objectives are powerful things, especially when linked (as they should be) to appraisal. Get them wrong and your whole organisation will go off in the wrong direction. Take particular care if you are tempted to define your objectives in monetary terms. This approach can sometimes be very effective. Equally, it can turn you all into novice accountants, quite oblivious to your wider or longer-term responsibilities. See also the advice on measurement in the section on planning, below.

Although the job plan should emphasise the importance of achieving worthwhile objectives, rather than the ability to demonstrate a range of grade-related skills or behaviour, it should also make it clear what levels of skill, effort and achievement represent satisfactory performance. This will help those who wish to show that their performance has been much better than satisfactory. It can also be useful to deploy the concept of 'breakthrough performance' when trying to explain the difference between what is in the civil service generally known as 'Box 2' rather than 'Box 3' (i.e. satisfactory) performance.

Although I always write the first draft of the person's objectives, the document obviously has to be shown in draft to the person being managed. In particular, I have often found it helpful to ask colleagues to say, in effect, what they offer to do by way of satisfactory performance. This can help dispel unreal expectations that satisfactory performance is somehow deserving of an exceptional report. Indeed, I take the firm view that Box 2 breakthrough performance cannot be recognised in the absence of a clear agreement between manager and managed which specifies the level of performance which has been exceeded.

Planning and Measurement

Having set your objectives, you must now plan how you will get there.

Planning is of course an unnatural process. After all, it is much more fun to do something. And the other nice thing about not planning is that failure comes as a complete surprise rather than being preceded by a period of worry and depression. But experienced managers know that planning is (a) relatively simple (which is perhaps another reason why it does not appeal to many civil servants) and (b) an indispensable precursor to success. The main thing, therefore, is to do it! But when you do it, these are the key points which need to be borne in mind:

- keep it simple;
- focus on results, i.e. what is to be achieved;
- ensure individual responsibility for all members of the team, preferably by managing through a structured breakdown of the project into constituent parts which are the responsibility of named individuals;
- communicate, and in particular clearly communicate both objectives and progress both within and outside the team;
- monitor progress both carefully and frequently.

Much of the above implies measurement. This lies at the heart of effective management, whether of the policy process or of anything else. We all know – though we often forget – that 'you cannot manage what you do not measure'. Another version of this saying is that 'If you measure it, you change it' - which leads to the conclusion that you should 'Make the important measurable, not the measurable important.' This really is the key to success in all your endeavours, and time spent on unmeasured activity is the most likely time to be wasted.

Morale

Civil servants often worry about the morale of their team, as if good morale is one of their objectives. This is almost always a mistake.

Morale, just like happiness, is surprisingly elusive. It is a great mistake to try directly to improve morale. Good morale comes naturally to any well-managed team, and never comes to a team that is poorly led, lacks clear objectives, is poorly trained or lacks good honest communication. So if you are lead and manage well, high morale will inevitably follow, however difficult the surrounding circumstances.

Do also bear in mind that morale will inevitably dip during a period of rapid change. The team does not at first realise that it needs to change. (This state is sometimes unkindly referred to as 'unconscious incompetence'.) Once it faces up to its problems then confidence and morale will inevitably decline ('conscious incompetence'). It will then begin to do better, although perhaps rather self-consciously ('conscious competence') and finally morale will rise rapidly once the new way of working has become second nature ('unconscious competence'). It is then the job of the leader to ensure that this state is maintained for as long as possible, through seeking continuous improvement, so that the team does not slip back into unconscious incompetence.

Managing Money

After your team, money is your next most important resource. As it is public money, you must constantly bear in mind three basic and unbreakable rules which are designed to prevent fraud:

- The person who authorised the expenditure (i.e. entered into the contract) can never ever be the same as the person that authorises the payment of the subsequent bill.
- Never pay a bill 'in advance of need', that is before the goods or services have been delivered and have been found to be satisfactory.
- If there is a limit to your financial authority (i.e. you have been told that you may only spend up to £xxxxx) you may not circumvent this by splitting contracts and bills into a number of smaller parts.

You may be tempted, especially towards a year end when you are anxious to spend your budget, to ignore one or more of these rules. You absolutely may never do so, on pain of dismissal, even if your intentions are honourable.

But there is much more to spending money sensibly than merely obeying the rules. After your staff, money is the other principal resource at your disposal as you seek to achieve your objectives. But will you use it as a Sop or Lever?

> *Money may be used as a sop, or it may be used as a lever. When you use it as a sop . . . you get some friendly notes in the press . . . but it is gone. But if you use it as a lever it may be made to influence matters of far greater consequence than is measured even by the actual amount involved*
>
> Sir Winston Churchill

These words are even more true today than when first written. It is all too easy for both Ministers and officials to kid themselves, and kid others, that they are doing good by spending money. This is particularly apparent at Party Conference time, when every announcement seems to have a price tag, and the larger the better.

I deal separately with the control of large scale projects and programmes, but offer the following thoughts on the sensible use of 'programme spend' – those budgets which are delegated to individual civil servants and often used to support those projects outside government which contribute to the Government's wide or narrow objectives.

It is of course very tempting to throw the Government's resources behind those seeking to 'do good'. But don't rush into a decision. The money will be wasted unless you ensure that the project is structured in such a way as to maximise the chances of it being successfully completed, and of its being good value for money. Pay particular attention to the following:

- Every project must have clear, worthwhile and testable objectives. ('Worthwhile' means that they make a difference in the real world. For example you should not merely pay for a conference to be held. You should stipulate that it must attract x delegates who must, after the conference, record that they have learned something or will take some action. In the case of larger projects you must ensure that there is, for example, a measurable change in competitiveness or behaviour.) And you must make it clear that no grant (or a reduced grant) will be paid if the objectives etc. are not achieved. You should in particular not spend a lot on programmes whose main purpose is to 'bring people together' (e.g. large and small firms, industry and academia). These objectives are laudable, but not worth tens of thousands of pounds, let alone millions. Far better, buy them all a nice lunch!

- Every project must be 100 per cent 'owned' outside Government. We may feel very committed to the work, but our role is to be a supporter and banker, not the entrepreneur or owner. The more we get involved, the more we risk reducing the sense of ownership, and hence the commitment, of the true project managers. In particular, every project must have a clear champion – one person outside Government who is personally committed to seeing it through to a successful conclusion. And there should be clear evidence that larger projects are backed by a senior figure who is unambiguously committed to exploiting the results of the project. We cannot afford to bankroll the ambitions or hunches of staff who are not fully backed by their directors.

- Remember in particular that you cannot give money to a body of which you are a member. If your job requires you to join a board which is supervising a programme or project, you must make it crystal clear that you are only doing so as an observer. Remember too the related point that you must not behave in such a way as to suggest that the Government might stand behind a body which is receiving public funds. If you were to do this, you might be deemed to have become a 'shadow director' in which case you might find that the taxpayer has become liable for the whole of the debts of the body concerned.

- Similarly, there should be clear evidence of financial commitment from outside Government. Be particularly wary if you are asked to pay more than 25 per cent of the cost of a project. This suggests that no-one else is willing to put much of their money where their mouth is. This is especially true of collaborative projects where the non-HMG proportion is shared between several participants, none of whom, it often turns out, are much bothered about whether the project succeeds.

- You should be particularly reluctant to accept that Government money might be necessary to 'pump prime' a project which will eventually stand on its own feet. You need to ask why someone should support the project once the pump has been primed, when they are not prepared to do so now.

- Take care if you are asked to support interesting experimental work in, say, one school or one company or one local authority area. If the experiment appears successful, are Ministers committed, and will the financial and managerial resources be available, to implement the change nationwide?

- You must set up robust monitoring arrangements (which will survive your moving on to another job) if money might need to be repaid to the Government after the final grant has been paid over. Examples include loan agreements and grants to create employment, which are repayable if the jobs disappear within X years.

Programme and Project Management

The words 'programme' and 'project' are, in most cases, inter-changeable. In theory, a programme is large scale, and often consists of a number of projects. But a project can be pretty big too, and can certainly appear very challenging to those in charge of it. Programmes and projects should therefore be managed in pretty much the same way, using the approach outlined below.

Before you do anything else, sit down and think hard about the following issues:

- What is the result you want to achieve?
- What are the causal factors that influence that result?
- What policy interventions will make a difference?
- What is the evidence?
- Who do you rely on to deliver?

You should also think hard, up front, about the following three critical factors for successful delivery

Critical Success Factor 1: The right scope:
- Any investment of time or money must linked to clear outcomes that support strategic objectives.
- Goals must be realistic and based on knowledge of what is achievable

Critical Success Factor 2: Adequate skills and resources:
- These must be matched to the demands of the programme/project

Critical Success Factor 3: Good processes for delivery
- Ensure that your delivery processes are based on approaches that are likely to work.

Planning for Delivery

Once you have thought long and hard about the above issues, and ensured that Ministers and other key stakeholders agree with your conclusions, you can settle down to detailed planning. The following are the nine main steps you should take to decide on the best way forward to achieve the outcome you want. You should prepare and circulate, including to Ministers, a detailed plan which answers each of the following questions. The questions are repeated and described in more detail in Annex 3. The detailed checklist can also be printed out from the civilservant.org.uk website.

1: What is the scope? What is to be delivered - and when?
2: What resources and capabilities (people, physical resources and funding) will you need?
3: What are the potential sources of such capabilities?
4: Who will carry out the required processes and policies?
5: Who will be accountable for what?
6: Which similar projects have succeeded – and why?
7: What is an acceptable balance of cost, benefit and risk?– and how should they be managed?
8: How you will work with other delivery agents and stakeholders to share information and knowledge?
9: How will you monitor and report progress? What performance measures and incentives will you need?

Last, but not least, consider whether your programme or project might not be affected by one of the most frequent causes of failure, which are:

• unclear objectives and success criteria;
• insufficient involvement of key stakeholders;

- weak risk management;
- unclear roles and responsibilities;
- lack of appropriate skills;
- weak financial control;
- poor market knowledge.

They won't happen to you? I wonder!

10   Personal Effectiveness

This final chapter summarises some other advice and training which I have found thought-provoking and useful.

Managing Time

This is an important skill. We have a duty to the taxpayer to work efficiently. And we all need to balance the demands of work, family and friends, as well as find time for ourselves – to get enough sleep, to relax and to pursue our own interests.

So why are we so often poor time managers? Perhaps we recognise that a good time manager is essentially lazy, and only does what is really important. We are all reluctant to appear lazy, even if this is a natural accompaniment to great efficiency. Nevertheless, it is worth following these rules:

Concentrate On Your Objectives and Don't Let Others Control Your Time. Do not be too reactive. It is important that you decide how to spend your time, and that you do not organise your time so as to please other people. First, cut out any activity which does not take you nearer to one of your objectives. For instance:

- Consider whether that meeting, lunch or conference is going to help you achieve your objectives. If not, don't go.
- Read what you need to know, not what it's nice to know. Is it

really likely that those papers will contain important new information? Will reading them take you nearer to one of your objectives? If not, don't read them.

- Do you get your hard information, such as statistics, direct from source? If so, why read endless commentaries on them? Take yourself off all those circulation lists.

- Consider whether it is really essential that the Minister should speak at, or attend, a particular event. Don't forget that you will in due course have to find the time to prepare briefing and write a speech.

- Consider whether you really do need to accompany the Minister.

Don't hesitate, when under pressure, to take control of your time by closing your door, borrowing an empty office, or working at home, in order to avoid interruption. Colleagues should be assured that they can disturb you if it is really necessary, but otherwise you should tell callers that you are 'a bit tied up at the moment'.

If you want a brief word with a colleague, go to see them so that you can bring the conversation to an end when you are ready, rather than wait for them to leave you. And if you want the discussion to be a short one, don't sit down!

Don't worry about refusing to go to a meeting which clashes with an important prior engagement. If the organiser had thought it vital that you were there, they would have first checked your availability. There is more of a problem if you want to be at the meeting, but the organiser does not much care whether or not you are there. You then have to decide which is the most important. But unless the second engagement is clearly more important, it is common courtesy to stick with your prior engagement.

If you do organise or attend a meeting, make sure there is a clear agenda, and decide in advance how much time the subject is worth. If the subject is of some interest to you, but not worth more than a few minutes of your time, ask the person chairing the meeting if you can attend for the key part of the discussion, or tell him or her that you have to leave in so many minutes. Or get someone else to attend on your behalf.

Indeed, the solution to many time management problems is to . . .

Empower your Colleagues.
Empowerment requires a certain amount of courage and patience. Work should generally be done by the most junior colleague that can be expected to do it properly, and find it stimulating. The only exceptions are non-repetitive tasks that you can do quickly and easily yourself. It then often takes less time to do it yourself than to tell someone else what needs to be done.

Few of us empower effectively. A significant proportion of what we do could generally be done by colleagues, if we were prepared to invest a little time in training and guidance. This investment of time can seem a burden if you are already under pressure, but the pay back can be amazingly quick. You will not only free up your own time, you will also improve the quality of your colleagues' jobs.

So now you are thoroughly lazy, but still have too much to do. You must now improve the way you organise your work. The essential first step is to . . .

Prioritise Your Activities.
It is in the nature of our work that 80 per cent of our results will come from 20 per cent of activities. It is therefore very helpful to prioritise your work fairly frequently. You should then concentrate on those tasks which are going to be the most effective in getting you closer to your objectives. Leave the lower priority tasks to later in the day, or tomorrow. By definition, it does not matter if you do not finish them today. You can then go home at a reasonable time, secure

in the knowledge that you have done your most effective work.

In prioritising your work, it is useful to decide whether it is (a) urgent and (b) important. If it is both urgent and important, you should do it as soon as possible. If it is urgent but not important, delegate it to someone else. If it is important and not urgent, do it later. If it is neither urgent nor important, don't do it!

Paper Handling.
A very good rule is to handle each piece of paper only once. For instance, if you read a letter, and know what you want to say in reply, dictate the reply straightaway. Otherwise you will just have to re-read the letter, and rethink the reply, on another occasion. Alternatively, delegate the paper to someone else, or throw it in the bin. The only paper that should be put on one side is that which is (a) important, (b) requires considerable thought, and (c) is not urgent.

Finally . . .

We All Procrastinate.
We therefore all need to adopt our own solution to this problem. Once you realise that you are putting off a difficult task, plan your campaign accordingly. Set aside a time and place to tackle it. Decide that you will not have lunch, or not go to bed, until you have done so. Spread the papers out. We each can develop our own individual technique. The important thing is to begin the process. You know very well that the task will appear much easier once you have started.

Managing Meetings

Meetings are ever-popular as a practical and convivial alternative to work. But if you are determined to run a successful and efficient meeting then the key, as ever, is proper planning.

If you will be chairing the meeting, take a minute or two to clarify the purpose of the meeting. What will have been achieved if the meeting has been successful? Also think carefully about who should attend. Attendance should be firmly linked to the purpose of the meeting. If a decision is to be taken, you need to invite only those who need to be committed to the decision. If it is a planning meeting, you need to invite only those who can bring important information and advice to the planning process. You should then make sure that everyone knows the purpose of the meeting, preferably by letting them have a short note in writing. This gives them an opportunity to suggest the names of others who might attend, or to suggest that they need not attend themselves.

If you are invited to a meeting, ensure that you understand the purpose of the meeting, if necessary by talking to the chairman, or the Private Secretary in the case of a meeting with a Minister. Then consider whether you really need to attend, in order to contribute information or to the discussion. Remember that it is seldom necessary for two people from the same team to attend a meeting which is not central to the objectives of that team. It saves a lot of time if only one person attends and reports the outcome to the other.

The Conduct Of The Meeting

Unless there is only one easily defined subject, there should be an agenda, preferably circulated in advance. The Chair should decide, at the beginning of the meeting, approximately how much time will be given to each agenda item, and should give this information to those attending. And unless the Chair is certain that everyone knows everyone else, all attending should be asked to give their name and division, department etc. In a large pre-orchestrated meeting, it is better to prepare name-plates.

Those introducing papers circulated before the meeting should assume that they have been read, and should therefore limit their comments to emphasising one or two key points, conclusions or recommendations.

A note of the discussion should not be prepared unless it will clearly be helpful either for those who were not at the meeting, or in order to record discussion, for public accountability reasons, of a particularly difficult issue. However, a note of action points must always be prepared and circulated to all present. The Chair should appoint someone to do this (or someone to take a full note if necessary) either before or at the beginning of the meeting. An electronic white board is particularly useful, because action points can be written down as they occur and in full view of everyone, and can then be printed off and distributed at the end of the meeting. Otherwise use a flip chart.

Follow-up

It is particularly important that names and time scales are attached to action points. And progress on all action points should either be reviewed at a further meeting on the same subject, or by the Chair or their nominee if no further meeting is to be held within an appropriate timescale.

Managing Negotiations

We spend much of our time in negotiations – trying to reach agreement with colleagues or those outside Government. The following advice should be borne in mind if the negotiations seem likely to be important or difficult.

[Note that this advice only applies when all the parties have a long-term relationship and want to reach a durable agreement which

159

fairly resolves conflicting interests. It does not apply when one party is merely consulting the other, nor when one party is not concerned about reaching an agreement, or is out to 'win', or will if necessary force through their chosen result.]

Planning

Thorough planning is essential. You need to think carefully about all aspects of the issue, and the likely concerns of the other parties, or you will be surprised and out-manoeuvred at each stage. Make sure in particular that you know all the relevant facts. Make sure, too, that you have a good idea of what drives your Minister and how they would react if they were at the negotiating table. Do you know the limits of your negotiating power? In what circumstances do you need to refer back to Ministers and/or others in Government?

You must establish your minimum and maximum requirements – i.e. the area within which you are free to negotiate. You must decide in advance that, if you do not reach your minimum requirements, you will have to walk away without agreement. Your minimum requirements should therefore be the result of a logical review of the situation in which you find yourself, and should be agreed with those to whom you are reporting. Try to avoid using the phrase 'bottom line'. This means different things to different people, and is often no more than the current limit of your negotiating brief, i.e. the point at which you have to report back to others. If there are no circumstances in which you can walk away from the negotiation, then you should be clear about this from the beginning.

Take time to examine the issue through the eyes of the other parties. In particular, what are their likely minimum and maximum requirements, including non-negotiables? Listen carefully to what they say during the negotiation. You need to identify areas of common ground so that you can have a negotiation which maximises the benefit to all the parties.

The Conduct of the Negotiation

You should set out to manage the process, ensuring that all the issues are identified and dealt with in a business-like way. Keep recording and reviewing what has been agreed so that there can be no misunderstanding, and so that the area of disagreement is steadily reduced.

Be up-front about non-negotiables but otherwise generally avoid being either 'tough' or 'nice'. The first, if met by toughness, will only lead to deadlock. The second will lead to your arriving at an unfair result, unless all the other parties also act nice – which is unlikely. Try to defuse heated argument. The best approach is usually to be sensitive to the other people, but resolute about the problem. If apparently deadlocked, consider offering a face-saver (without going below your minimum requirements). Or be creative. Surprise the other parties by coming at the issue in a totally different way.

Finally, and this is important, always call a short adjournment when you appear to have reached agreement but before settling on it. You need to reflect on what you have agreed to make sure that it is sensible, fair and consistent with your negotiating brief. You also need to ensure that you have dealt with all the issues and have not left any uncertainties or ambiguities.

Managing Personal Relationships

Here are a few techniques that can be used if you feel that you are not getting on with, or not getting through to, someone with whom you are dealing.

First, pay attention to the need for clear communication. Use simple unambiguous language, and explain the reasons for your proposals or requirements. Never get angry and always be polite (but not unctuous). Remember that aggressive and demanding people often have fairly thick skins. And obsessive people often feel that something is being hidden from them. Tell both sorts of person that you intend, if they agree, not to beat about the bush. They will always agree and then you can deal with any problem in blunt terms.

Next, pay attention to your relative status. We all communicate with each other as superiors, equals or inferiors and we frequently adopt different approaches to the same person at different times. Problems invariably arise, in work as well as at home, when one party's approach does not meet the expectations of the other.

The usual starting point in any analysis of expectations is that we all expect to be treated with respect, and with due recognition of our different skills, experiences and perspectives. For instance, we should not talk down to Ministers (although some colleagues seem to forget this) or to the public (ditto) and Ministers should not talk down to us. Sometimes, however, this approach needs to be abandoned. For instance, you may need to defer to a Minister or manager, e.g. if time is short, or if he or she clearly has much more experience or knowledge than you, or if he or she has already heard enough and wants you to accept their decision. The need for you to do so is usually signalled pretty clearly. If you are slow to notice the signals then problems will certainly follow. Equally, excessive use of deference can also cause problems. Ministers, managers and the public expect to deal, most of the time, with experienced professional civil servants. Lengthy displays of deference will cause them to write you off as inferior in ability as well as status.

So if your relationship with someone seems to be fraught or distant, or if you suspect that they actively dislike you, consider carefully whether you are signalling superiority, equality or inferiority when they are expecting something else. It is then usually best if you change your approach to meet the expectations of the other, but it might be necessary to signal strongly to the other person that you expect them to adopt a different approach when dealing with you.

Finally, we need to work with people as they really are, not as we would wish them to be. We are each, to different extents, extrovert, introvert, practical, creative, analytical, driven by beliefs, flexible and structured. Some people will be quite different from you, and you will think them decidedly odd. You must put all this on one side when assessing whether the person concerned is talking sense and acting effectively. But you should learn to go further and to some extent adapt your own behaviour to the character of the person with whom you are dealing. If you proudly treat everyone in the same way, you are certainly not dealing effectively with many of them.

Whose Problem Is It?

This should be the first question you ask when you are be faced with a task, problem or issue which seems particularly complex, hard to handle or embarrassing. It is surprising how often a few moments analysis can lead you to break the problem down into manageable pieces, each to be dealt with by separate people. Indeed, you will often find that the underlying problem does not belong to you, or your Minister, in the first place, whereupon you can relax! A few examples might help:

- If you are concerned about the performance of one of your staff then the problem, in the final analysis, is theirs rather than yours. It is for you, not them, to set standards – that is why you have been asked to manage their work. It may be that your colleague can convince you that you have not given them full credit for certain aspects of their work. Or they might tell you about a temporary problem (e.g. health or domestic difficulties) that is affecting their performance. Failing that, they must either change or improve if they are to avoid the consequences of your concern. Of course the colleague might transfer the problem back to you e.g. by explaining that they are not clear about their objectives, or persuading you they do not have the right resources. But now you have something to fasten on to and the step by step identification of the owner of the problem can lead to its resolution.

- If someone applies for some sort of permission, or financial support, and provides insufficient information, or information which suggests that it should be refused, then again the problem is theirs, not yours. You must be prepared to say 'No' and not wimp out by asking further questions. Of course you should also explain the nature of the difficulty so that the company or person can decide whether to commit resource to overcoming your objection. But you must make it clear that the decision to do so is theirs, not yours. For goodness sake do not appear to encourage them to do lots of work flexing an application which is almost bound to fail.

- Much the same applies to the person who presses for a quick decision, before you have been able to carry out the necessary consultations or checks. If it is truly impossible to consider the case properly in the time available, you should simply explain that the current decision would be unfavourable. It is for them to decide whether to require you to meet their deadline, or to extend it. (And it is surprising how often they do the latter.)

- And if you are waiting for a task to be completed, or for money or information, the problem is the provider's, not yours. You should get the provider to give you a definite date by which it will appear, beyond which they know that you will hold them responsible for any consequences. The date is then their problem and they can hardly complain if you take unwelcome action after they have failed to meet a deadline which they themselves have set. And it is much better to accept one distant deadline than be forced into giving frequent extensions.

Further Information and Developments

The website which supports this book (www.civilservant.org.uk) contains a good deal of more detailed advice and information, including about:

- the definition of 'civil servant'
- the range of public bodies for which civil servants work
- working with scientists and scientific issues, including risks to health and safety.

For those who want to read further, it is also well worth looking at the Directory of Civil Service Guidance, which is, despite its name, a surprisingly accessible two-part publication which covers everything from 'Access by Former Ministers to Official Papers' through to 'Whistleblowing'. It is available free from the Cabinet Office (020 7276 2474) or the Cabinet Office website. I also recommend Whitehall by Peter Hennessy, which provides a comprehensive introduction to the history, structure, strengths and weaknesses of Whitehall. And, as I do not seek to describe the role of the civil servants who work very close to the Prime Minister, those interested in this tiny but important part of the civil service are recommended to read Kavanagh & Seldon's The Powers behind the Prime Minister. The best book on media handling, in my view, is Nicholas Comfort's How to Handle the Media.

Much of this book describes professional practices and constraints which, for good reason, have changed very little over recent years.

But it also deals with a number of areas which have been subject to rapid change, and where change might well continue. These areas include Parliamentary procedures, human rights, freedom of information and devolution. Change may also result from the Civil Service Reform programme.

Such changes will be recorded on the web-site (www.civilservant.org.uk) which accompanies this book, as will any errors in the book and new information. I would therefore be extremely grateful for comments on the book, for information about relevant developments, and for suggestions about further subjects which might be included on the web-site. These should be sent to:

Martin.Stanley@civilservant.org.uk

or to

Martin Stanley
c/o Politico's Publishing
215 Vauxhall Bridge Road
London SW1V 1EJ

Appendix I: Replies to Invitations

Replies to unsigned invitation cards follow the standard form of words set out below, and neither the Minister nor the Private Secretary signs the reply:

> *Mr . . . thanks the President of the Worshipful Company of Toast Fork Manufacturers for her kind invitation to the reception on . . . [and is glad to accept] or [but regrets that he is unable to attend].*

Letters declining invitations to specific events usually start by thanking the correspondent 'for his/her kind invitation to', or ' for kindly inviting me to', the event.

There then follows one of a range of possible formulations, depending on the underlying reason for the refusal. Similar formulations can sometimes be used to decline invitations to, say, write magazine articles. But you should always avoid dishonesty. It has a nasty habit of being detected.

Some examples, for Ministerial or Private Secretary signature, are as follows:

Standard refusals:

> *However, as I am sure you will appreciate, the Minister receives many requests of this kind and cannot accommodate them all.*

She therefore regrets that she must decline your invitation on this occasion.

Or:

. . . but sadly, pressures on her diary are such that she is unable to accept.

Or:

Regretfully I must decline. As you can imagine, I receive many invitations from a number of excellent candidates but cannot, unfortunately, respond positively to them all.

Or:

As I am sure you will appreciate, I receive many invitations of this kind. I am sorry that I have to decline your invitation on this occasion.

If the invitation is in respect of a particularly busy period:

Unfortunately, due to heavy diary commitments around that time, I am unable to accept your invitation.

Or:

Unfortunately his diary is particularly full during the period in question and he therefore regrets that he will be unable to accept your invitation.

If there is a definite prior engagement:

> *Unfortunately I [have a prior engagement] [will be abroad at the time] and so must regretfully decline your invitation.*

But if you have checked that another Minister is willing to take on the engagement and that the substitution is probably acceptable to the hosts, the Minister might add:

> *However, I understand that [another Minister] would be glad to address the conference. If this would be acceptable, perhaps your secretary could contact his diary secretary (tel: 020 7 . . .) to confirm the arrangements.*

A refusal to have a further meeting with those interested in a familiar subject (drafted in this case for either Prime Ministerial or Private Secretary reply) might read:

> *As you know, [Ministers] met . . . on . . . [and are fully aware of the importance of this subject to your constituents]. And they are keeping in close touch with developments. [I] [They] do not therefore think that there would be any practical value in holding an additional meeting.*

If appropriate, the letter can be rounded off with best wishes for the success of the event. Examples are:

> *However, I hope that the dinner is a great success.*

Or:

*The Minister was, however, pleased to note . . . And has asked
me to send you his [congratulations and] good wishes for the
future.*

Or:

*She would however like to send her best wishes for what she
hopes will be [a] [an interesting and] successful event.*

It can be more difficult to decline a general invitation e.g. to visit a
company when next in the area. But the Minister might use one of
the standard refusals at (a) above or, if true, simply say:

I have no plans to visit the area in the near future

But if the Minister means it, he or she might add:

*. . . but if I [am] [or another Minister is] in the area [I will]
[we shall] certainly bear [the company] in mind.*

Or a Private Secretary might add:

*He will certainly keep the company in mind for inclusion in a
future visit to the area if possible.*

(But note that the use of either of these formulations will require the
appropriate Government Office to make an effort to include the
company in a future visiting programme.)

Appendix II: A Policy Checklist

The following is a useful checklist which encapsulates much of the advice in this book about policy development – and more besides. A copy of this checklist can be down-loaded from www.civilser-vant.org.uk.

Good policies have the following characteristics:

- They specify the real world outcomes they were designed to achieve, and the outputs necessary along the way.
- They are based on a thorough understanding of the situation Ministers want to change, why it had proved resistant to any previous efforts to make a difference, and the likely dynamics of bringing change about.
- They are based on evidence, using data sources both within the department and across the research community, and also taking account of international experience accessed through visits, dialogue, the Internet and symposia.
- Each policy should clearly fit within the overall government and departmental strategy, and its contribution to meeting Ministerial goals and targets should be clearly specified.
- Ministers should have been involved early in the policy process, across a number of departments where appropriate, and involving key players both within the department and outside experts when brainstorming ideas.
- End users, delivery partners and other key stakeholders should be

involved in policy development alongside colleagues right across the department and elsewhere in Whitehall, to develop strategies which are workable, linked, innovative and in line with best practice across the world.

- There should be effective use of widespread consultation, utilising the latest techniques and approaches, including the People's Panel.
- There should be a thorough appraisal of alternatives (including the most radical – and including doing nothing).
- Evaluation should be built in from inception, through delivery to outputs, with regular feedback, to ensure the policy stays focused on the outcomes it aimed to achieve.
- Communication and presentation are integrated into, and seen as critical to the success of, the whole of the policy process.
- All significant consequences – including unintended consequences – are taken into account. Particular care must be taken to consider diversity/equality issues and the impact on business and the environment, and also make sure that you think 'outside the box' – will your programme improve the problem or merely shift it elsewhere?
- The policy process should be managed using project management techniques (e.g. setting a clear timetable; planning for interdependencies; identification of necessary resources, both financial and human; risk analysis and contingency planning).
- Policies should be deliverable, and implemented with determination and persistence as to the key principles and objectives, but with a willingness to pilot, learn and adapt as to the practical details in the light of experience.
- There should be benchmarking of the policy process against the best across Whitehall and beyond.
- Service delivery should be designed around the needs of end-users, rather than departmental bureaucracies, or the

convenience of delivery institutions.
* We should make the most effective use of technologies – for example the Internet – to design, consult on and deliver policies, to link government to intermediaries, and to the citizen.

Appendix III: Delivery Planning Checklist

These are the nine main decisions you need to take as you plan a major project or programme.

For convenience, the steps are described in a sequence; in practice, you will revisit some of the steps as your available choices become clear.

1: Determine the scope: what to deliver and when

- Describe why the work needs to be done – for example, to meet a policy imperative or respond to a business driver for change.
- Describe the required outcome in measurable, time based terms – what you want to change and how you will know that you have changed it.
- Identify high level benefits, how they contribute to strategic objectives and how they will be measured. Identify the causal factors – what needs to be in place for the outcome to happen?
- Describe the actions/projects that need to be undertaken.
- Identify high level options for meeting the business need; identify the option with the most acceptable mix of cost, benefit and risk.

2: Estimate the resources and capabilities (people, physical resources and funding) you will need

- Base your estimates on what others have done, wherever possible.
- Look at the dependencies between current programmes and

projects in your organisation to arrive at the optimum allocation of resources.

- Establish the skills and expertise you need (capability to do the job) and the numbers of people who will be required over the lifetime of the project (capacity).
- Estimate the whole-life cost of the change – people and physical resources (buildings, technology etc).
- Consider whether your organisation has enough experience and skills to manage new arrangements where they involve working with others.
- Determine the budget/resource limits and where the costs will fall.

3: Identify potential sources of capability

- Investigate who could deliver the required outcome. Look at the whole supply chain – your organisation, business partners, suppliers and their suppliers, your advisers and your customers.
- Consider innovative ways of delivery, such as collaborating with the private sector where there are appropriate incentives for them to do so.
- Look at what others are doing.
- Where relevant, look at opportunities to exploit technology to deliver the capability you need.

4: Decide who will carry out the required processes and policies

- Look at the proposed way/s forward in the context of the business, its current portfolio and priorities; check that they fit with the organisation's strategy.
- Check for opportunities to collaborate with others and for

overlaps with projects already planned or underway; look at the interfaces with other initiatives/organisations.

- Establish how much is new or changing in terms of people and the way they work, services and physical resources such as buildings and IT. Make a realistic assessment of the likelihood of success, given your organisation's existing commitments, priorities, capability and capacity.
- Consider whether critical business processes would be affected
- Consider breaking the work down into smaller packages instead of doing everything at once.
- Revisit the priorities; in addition, expect the unexpected – could you cope with unforeseen change?

5: Determine who will be accountable for what

- Establish who will be responsible for making investment decisions (for example, the board, partners) and who will be senior individual responsible for the project/programme as its owner.
- Check that the right person is given the role, in terms of their authority and responsibilities in relation to the proposed change.
- Define high level governance structures and responsibilities; consider how different responsibilities fit together and how everyone involved will understand their role and responsibility.
- Define high level arrangements for reporting downwards on policy and business requirements, reporting upwards on progress, performance and risks and taking prompt action as required.
- For joint projects, identify the additional arrangements that need to be in place.
- Ensure that reporting lines will be kept as short as possible.

6: Identify similar projects that have succeeded

- Compare your project with other ways of delivering a similar outcome – public/private sector and internationally.
- Take account of factors that could affect success, such as cultural differences.
- Identify why others have succeeded – or failed – and the lessons learned from their experiences.

7: Determine an acceptable balance of cost, benefit and risk – and how they should be managed

- Confirm the solution that offers best value for money; obtain approval from senior management.
- Revisit the key risks to performance and delivery. Risks relating to performance could include lack of public interest leading to poor take-up of a service; risks relating to performance could include overambitious timescales, inadequate resources and lack of essential skills.
- Consider the whole supply chain, including intermediaries, and how risks could be allocated and managed.
- For the proposed way forward, identify an acceptable balance of costs, benefits and risk.
- Consider a wide range of possibilities and the tradeoffs associated with each.
- If it is an innovative approach, consider how to manage the risks and how well your organisation could cope with the scale of change proposed by more radical options.
- Establish that each of the proposed options are practical, realistic and viable; consider how well each option meets stakeholder needs.
- Contingency plans need to be outlined at this stage.

8: Determine how you will work with other delivery agents and stakeholders to share information and knowledge

- Consider who your stakeholders are and what they want – the people who will be involved in/affected by the change and/or influence the outcome.
- Resolve any conflicting demands.
- Think about how you will achieve stakeholder buy-in and overcome any resistance to the change.
- Consider the perceptions that might have to change and how behaviours could be changed.

9: Determine arrangements for monitoring and reporting progress. Identify the performance measures and incentives you will need

- Set milestones – that is, progress checkpoints at specified intervals – against intermediate targets towards the required outcome. These milestones will enable you to track progress against plans and take action on any feedback relating to progress.
- Identify performance measures that are SMART (specific, measurable, achievable, realistic and time-based); determine mechanisms for reliable and regular performance information.
- Think about the incentives for staff, partners and suppliers that will encourage a successful outcome.
- Check that performance information can be collected efficiently and in good time to take remedial action if required.

accommodation: free 113

Index